D1571829

Mountain Wildflowers
of
Northern New Mexico
A Beginner's Guide

J. Rush Pierce
Amanda Pierce

JRP Publications

Mountain Wildflowers of Northern New Mexico. A Beginner's Guide

JRP Publications, Granbury, Texas

Printed by Taylor Publishing Co., Dallas, Texas

ISBN 0-9707640-0-6

Photos by J. Rush Pierce

This book is dedicated to -

Read, Rebecca, Sarah, Cason, Michael, Susanna

*They continue to inspire us, teach us, and
give us hope and joy.
They are the face of the future.*

'Consider the lilies of the field, how they grow;
They toil not, neither do they spin;
And yet I say unto you, that even Soloman in all his glory
Was not arrayed like one of these.'

Sometime in May the Sangre de Christo high country begins to awaken from its long winter's sleep. As the snows recede the springs, streams, and rivers burst forth with a profusion of cascading water. First the willows, then the aspens sprout their leaves and this is followed by the sudden appearance of grasses and shrubs in the meadows and glades; even the forest floor begins to produce a myriad of plants. Within a brief interval of time the landscape takes on a fresh bright greenish hue which stands against the darker cast of the evergreens. All of this is in contrast to the deep blue skies containing a multitude of brilliant white cumulus clouds. In June, onto this canvas background, suddenly appear dabs of red, blue, pink, and yellow which quickly grow, merge, and coelesce to form the brilliant color portrait of the summer mountains in full flower.

High mountain wildflowers appear to be brighter, more colorful, more vivid than their counterpoints found elsewhere. There must be several reasons for this but one of them is the exceptional light--the striking New Mexico light. Several decades ago D. H. Lawrence wrote an essay in which he paid homage to this special light and pointed out its influence as a magnet for artists. He reflected that somehow this light has a way of focusing the eye downward toward the earth itself and enhancing the rich colors of its beauty.

New Mexico light seems to occur in two very different forms. There is evening or desert light, of a pink or slightly lavender hue, which accentuates the earth tones and accounts in part for the beautiful desert sunsets. On the other hand, there is morning or mountain light, having a golden cast, which enhances the bright primary colors. It is this light which has something to do with the brilliance and richness of the mountain wildflowers.

From the beginning of time humans have maintained a long love affair with wildflowers, collecting and cultivating them, using them in celebrations and ceremonies, and attributing to them magical and mystical powers; certain flowers have been used for food while others have been valued as remedies for a variety of ills. This special attraction that we have for flowers goes down very deep into the human soul and has been observed in all human cultures, so that it almost seems innate. One could speculate about some of the reasons for this particular connection, for it must be more than the beauty, the colors, the intricate symmetry of the flowers. Part of it might be the fragrance, the aroma, the odor of wildflowers, for it is clear that the olfactory sense produces greater recall, a greater sense of *deja vu,* than our other senses. Some of it might simply be the realization by early people that flowers are a part of nature's calendar and can be used to herald and mark the seasons. Then there is the deeper understanding that the wildflowers call us to a basic perception of life, death, and re-birth, to a deep sense of our own mortality and yet our power of renewal. On some primitive level we realize that the cycle of flowers mimics our own, and from this we can draw a renewed understanding of the mysterious system of nature.

We hope that this book in some small way will call you to a renewal of this fundamental union with the wildflowers and bring you closer to all of nature.

If you are already a wildflower enthusiast or expert, this is not the book for you. There are other books available which are much more complete and detailed, identifying many varieties and species of flowers, both rare and common. This book is not for the initiated, but instead is for beginners and amateurs, those who may enjoy the beauty of wildflowers but cannot identify or name them. Therefore, the book should be thought of as an introduction to the mountain wildflowers.

Both of us are amateurs also and not being botanists, we have had little knowledge of this particular science and very little experience in dealing with it. Since this description conforms to that of the average person, we decided to produce a wildflower book for people like us, beginners and novices, those with little experience in flower identification and little knowledge of botany. Thus the book is designed to be as simple and straightforward as possible without a great deal of technical or scientific information

As a first step we decided to limit the number of flowers, for there are entirely too many for the beginner to learn easily. A more manageable number was arbitrarily chosen, about a hundred, and this includes the common and showy ones, especially those seen along roadsides, by-ways, and trails. We decided to also include a number of wildflowers that are less abundant but are unique and distinctive in color or appearance and therefore are easy to identify and remember. By including those flowers that are either common or unique, it is hoped that most of the wildflowers in the book can be identified from the photographs alone, without resorting to the descriptions.

Much of botany has to do with names and classification. Flowers are divided into Families which are broken down into groups (with Genus names) and then into sub-groups (or species). All of this is rather inexact so that at times there are differences even among experts concerning how a given flower should be classified. For this reason various flower books may differ over the specific name or the grouping of a particular specimen. We decided to stick to common names, especially descriptive names, since these are easier to learn and remember. Somewhere in the text we have listed the scientific names but in general the emphasis is on what is common and descriptive. Likewise, an effort has been made to avoid using the many technical terms that are found in flower description, and instead to rely on simple, descriptive language. An exception to this is the necessary use of some official names of the parts of flowers, but these are few and are covered in the Glossary.

Most flowers have a variety of different types and species which further complicates identification. Therefore in this book we have described only the most common forms. Exceptions to this are made in the few instances where more than one species is commonly found and then both are noted.

For beginners the easiest first step in identification is by color and the book is arranged in this fashion. It is obvious that some flowers are multi-colored, but stick to the predominant color and this should work. Some wild-flowers occur in several colors but we have tried to illustrate the most common variety while explaining in the text what other colors might be encountered. The book is divided into the following colors: red (including orange), pink (includes light purple), blue (includes dark purple), white, and yellow. The reds and blues are fairly easy while the yellow flowers are hardest to learn and differentiate because they are so numerous and similar.

Most of the flowers in the book should be easy to identify because of their distinctive appearance and should be recognized from the photographs alone. In order to make things a little more realistic, where possible, two pictures of each flower are included. One is relatively close up for better identification and the other is a more distant view (a "field view") showing the flowers as you might see them in passing by. This should give you a better idea of their actual size and habitat.

Unfortunately, botany is a rather dry subject so in order to add interest and flavor, the book includes some varied information about each of the wildflowers. For instance, there may be stories or legends about the flower's origin or something about the source of its name. Then there is the fact that some flowers have been honored in history (such as the rose) and a bit of this interesting information is included. Moreover, many of the more common flowers have been celebrated in literature so some of these references have been noted. Lastly, many of the flowers have been used in the past for practical purposes, medicinal and otherwise, and this information has also been added. All of this should make your wildflower search more interesting and enable you to more easily remember particular flowers.

The geographic area included in the book is North Central New Mexico, specifically the Sangre de Christo Mountains (most of the photographs were taken in Taos and Colfax counties). Of course, many of these flowers are found in other parts of the Rocky Mountains and some are very widespread. Therefore the book serves as a beginner's guide to many of the common wildflowers of the Western mountains. However, those plants found in arid or desert regions (such as cacti) and those found below 6,000 feet are not included.

TIPS

1. Any wildflower search must be done on foot and you must be willing to leisurely wander. Keep an eye out for any patch of color and examine it

closely. After identifying the plant, stop, move about and look closely for other flowers. The chances are that you will discover several other wildflowers you had not noticed. This is especially true when searching along roadsides.

2. When you find a flower try to match it with a photo in the book using the predominant color. If there is some uncertainty, look under the description of the flower and identification should be easy.

3. Remember that the book contains a limited number of wildflowers so you will not be able to identify all the flowers you may find.

4. Although the book is designed to be as non-technical as possible, there are a few terms with which you need to be familiar, especially the somewhat strange names of certain flower parts and leaf structures. This is covered in the Glossary so get acquainted with it.

5. For each flower there is listed the Family name and the botanical name (in this case the Genus name). Should you desire to look up a given plant in another wildflower book, it will be helpful to use these names.

6. Make it a habit to examine the entire plant especially the leaves. This will be very helpful should you decide to graduate to the rarer flowers or the many varieties and species. Flowers are scientifically divided according to *structure* and this may include the entire plant -- stems, leaves, roots as well as petals, sepals, stamens, and pistils. Examine the leaves in particular as these can be very helpful in identification. Look under the wildflower description and check the Glossary.

7. Be patient and examine the flowers carefully. They are not always what they seem at first glance. Some of the dual pictures (closeup and field view) help to emphasize this.

8. Remember that all the flowers shown here will not be blooming at the same time. Some appear in early spring (May), others in mid-summer or even in early fall (September). In the descriptive part of the text will be a note of the general blooming season for each particular flower.

9. With a little effort most all the flowers in the book can be found in a single season (almost all of the photographs were made during one summer). What you must be willing to do is to make frequent treks into the world of nature, pay close attention, keep a sharp eye, and be patient.

alternate - leaves not opposite each other.

anther - the part of the stamen which contains pollen.

basal leaves - leaves arising at the base of the plant.

bract - a modified leaf at the base of the flower.

calyx - the sepals, collectively.

compound leaf - two or more leaflets on a single leaf stalk.

corolla - the petals, collectively.

dentate - toothed.

disk - the central part of a composite flower, containing tiny disk flowers (as the central disk of a sunflower).

filament - the stalk of the stamen.

lanceolate leaves - lance shaped or lance-like leaves.

lancinate - cut into narrow segments.

leaflet - one of the leaves of a compound leaf.

linear leaves - long, narrow leaves with parallel sides.

lobed leaf - a leaf with the margins cut part way to the center with the outer parts rounded.

opposite leaves - pairs of leaves opposite one another.

oval or ovate leaves - leaves elliptic in shape.

palmate leaf - compound leaf with leaflets radiating like fingers.

pinnate leaf - compound leaf with leaflets arranged on each side of the leafstalk.

pistal - the ovule-bearing part of the plant, consisting of the ovary, stigma, and style.

rayflowers (rays) - the petals of a composite flower that surround the central disk (as the petals of a sunflower)

rhizome - a horizontal underground stem which can produce new flower stalks.

rosette - a cluster of leaves in a circular shape at the base of the plant.

sepal - a modified leaf below and outside the flower petals.

spike - a long flower cluster near the top of the stem with stalkless flowers.

stamen - the pollen-bearing organ of the plant consisting of the filament and anther.

stigma - the part of the pistal which is fertilized by pollen.

style - the part of the pistal connecting the stigma and ovary.

toothed leaf - tooth-like projections on the leaf margins.

umbel - a flower cluster (flat or convex) in which all the stems arise from a common point.

SEE NEXT PAGES

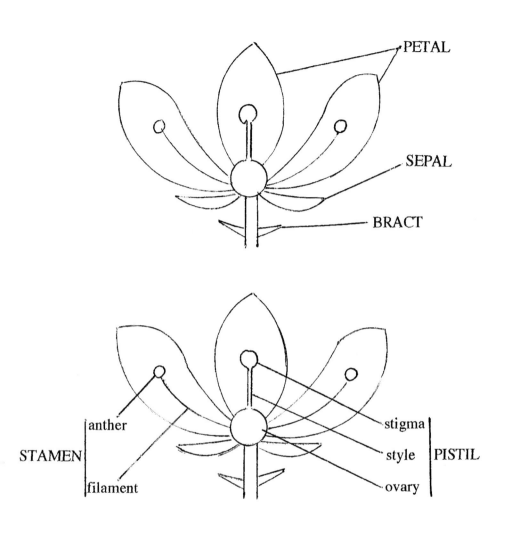

PETAL

SEPAL

BRACT

STAMEN | anther

filament

stigma | PISTIL

style

ovary

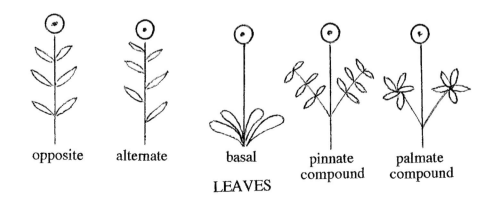

opposite   alternate   basal   pinnate compound   palmate compound

LEAVES

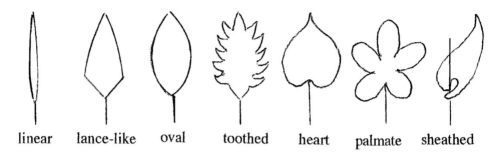

linear lance-like oval toothed heart palmate sheathed

LEAVES

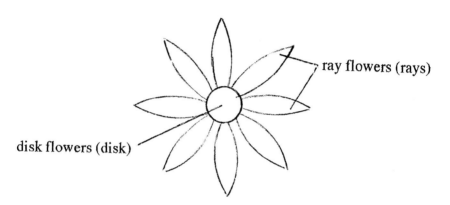

ray flowers (rays)

disk flowers (disk)

COMPOSITE FLOWER

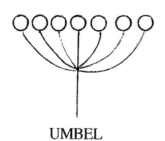

UMBEL

HABITATS

The following are various lists of flowers by their common habitats. These selections are somewhat inexact and are arbitrary, for many wildflowers are highly adaptable and can grow under a variety of conditions. However, in order to avoid multiple listing we have chosen the more common and well-recognized habitats and have used a variety of flower book sources for reference. Where there are differences of opinion, we have located the flower in those sites where we have actually located the individual specimens. More specifically, those habitats were chosen depending upon where the photographs were taken.

Meadows and fields -

blue flax	clover	salsify	sneezeweed
chicory	milkweed	mariposa lily	St. Johns wort
chimingbell	onion	white campion	sunflower
gentian	loco	yarrow	yellow primrose
harebell	thistle	butter and eggs	yellow paintbrush
iris	fairy trumpet	cinquefoil	wallflower
lupine	firewheel	dandelion	
penstemon	Mexican hat	nodding groundsel	
oxeye daisy	chickweed	California corn lily	

Open woods -

columbine	death camas	hollygrape
geranium	green gentian	parry lousewort
rose	strawberry	
Indian paintbrush	bracted lousewort	
Canada violet	goldenrod	

Deep forest -

Jacob's ladder	baneberry
fairy slipper	thimbleberry
coralroot	arnica
red columbine	

Wet areas, marshes, along streams -

larkspur	parry primrose	marsh marigold
monkshood	bog orchid	white checkermallow
elephanthead	brookcress	monkeyflower
shooting star	cow parsnip	

Dry, disturbed soil -

aster	evening primrose	gromwell
fireweed	sandwort	mullein
pink plume	butterweed	tasselflower
pussytoes	King's crown	yellow stonecrop
globemallow	golden smoke	

BLUE FLOWERS
Including dark purple flowers

BLUE FLAX

Family - Flax Family
Botanical name - *Linum Lewisii*
Season - June to early August

Description -
　Stems grow 1-2 feet high, are very fragile, lean and move in the slightest breeze. Flowers are produced along the stem and bloom singly from the bottom up. The flowers are 1 inch across, sky-blue, with 5 petals that are veined with purple. Leaves are numerous, very narrow, grass-like, and 1/2-1 inch across.

CHICORY

Family - Sunflower Family
Botanical name - *Chichorium*
Season - July to September

Description -
　The plant is 1-4 feet high with stems that are almost leafless and are heavily branched. The flower heads are 1-2 inches across and light blue with petals that are notched at the end. There are basal leaves which spread along the ground.

BLUE FLAX

This is a beautiful blue flower that appears in June and can almost cover the meadows and roadsides. It is also known as Lewis Flax, named for Meriwether Lewis.

Flax is one of the oldest of all textile fibers, some species having been cultivated for hundreds of years as a source of the fiber used in making linen. This fabric has been found in ancient Egyptian tombs and was manufactured extensively throughout the Roman Empire. Flax is also cultivated for its seeds from which linseed oil is extracted. The Latin word for flax, *linum,* serves as the root word for linen, linseed, and lingerie.

Each stem produces several flowers which bloom from the bottom up, one at a time. Flowers tend to fall off after only a day or two, but are replaced the following day. The stems are difficult to break and behave like string because of the tough fibers within.

An extract of the seeds was used at one time for colds, cough, fever, and urinary disorders; a poultice was thought to be helpful in gout, rheumatism and various types of inflammation.

CHICORY

Many of us are familiar with chicory as an additive to coffee, but few realize that this plant produces beautiful blue flowers. The plant is large, growing to 3 or 4 feet and consists of many-branched stems on which are found an array of sky-blue flowers. From a distance, the wildflower may be confused with blue flax, but close inspection will reveal that this is a composite flower that is lighter in color and slightly larger. The rays (or petals) are blunt and notched at the tips.

It is found in fairly dry soil, especially in meadows, fields and along the roadsides. An unusual feature is the fact that this flower opens in the early morning (around 5 or 6 A.M.) and closes by noon.

The roots can be roasted, ground into powder, and brewed with coffee to give the typical chicory flavor (1 1/2 tsp. of ground chicory per cup of coffee). In addition, the young stems and leaves can be eaten raw in salads.

CHIMINGBELL

Family - Borage Family
Botanical name - *Mertensia*
Season - June to August

Description -
Flowers are blue, drooping, bell-shaped and about 1 inch long. The Lanceleaf plant is short, about 12 inches tall, and has narrow, lance shaped leaves. The Tall Chimingbell is a large, leafy plant which grows to 4 feet, and has wide leaves.

COLORADO COLUMBINE

Family - Buttercup Family
Botanical name - *Aquilegia caerulea*
Season - June to August

Description -
The flower grows 8-24 inches on a long single stem. There are 5 bluish, star-like sepals in contrast to the 5 rounded white petals and the basal portion of each petal extends backward forming 5 slender spurs. Leaves are compound with cleft, lobed leaflets, and are mostly basal on the long stem.

CHIMINGBELL

Chimingbells are also known as Cowslips or Mountain Bluebells. Be careful about the use of the term bluebell because this name is also (and more appropriately) used for an entirely different flower, the Mountain Harebell. Chimingbells come in two common forms, the Tall Chimingbells and the Lanceleaf Chimingbells. The flowers of both are quite similar, the difference being in the size of the plant and the shape of the leaves. Chimingbell flowers are quite small and consist of light blue, drooping, bell-shaped blossoms. The unopened flowers often have a slight pink cast.

The Lanceleaf variety is found more commonly in dry, open areas while the Tall Chimingbell grows in damp areas and along the streams. Both varieties serve as forage for elk, deer, bear, and marmots. Pikas collect the plants and store them as hay for winter food.

COLORADO COLUMBINE

The Colorado or Blue Columbine is not only one of the most beautiful of all wildflowers, its unique appearance makes identification easy. This blue and white flower with its long spurs pointing backward is common throughout the Rocky Mountains and is the state flower of Colorado. The columbine is usually found between 8,000 and 12,000 feet in wet shaded areas, especially along the streams. It also appears among rocks, boulders, and in crannies, unexpected places for so exquisite a wildflower. The flower is said to be more colorful at higher altitudes.

The long spurs serve as reservoirs for nectar and make pollination easier.

The word columbine comes from the Latin word *columba* and means dove-like. In old paintings this flower represented the dove of peace. The botanical name (*Aquilegia*) also derives from Latin and the meaning is not clear. Some suggest it means eagle while others interpret it to mean water container or water collector.

GENTIAN

Family - Gentian Family
Botanical name - *Gentiana*
Season - July to September

Description -

The plant grows 4-18 inches tall with flowers single (Fringed Gentian) or several (Mountain Gentian) on a stem. Flowers are 1-2 inches across and the leaves are opposite, being oval (Mountain Gentian) or fairly narrow (Fringed Gentian).

HAREBELL

Family - Bluebell Family
Botanical name - *Campanula*
Season - June to August

Description -

The plant grows to 2 feet and the flowers, growing out of a slender stem, are dark blue to purplish-blue, and are in the shape of a hanging bell. The individual blossoms are 3/4 to 1 inch across and the petals are fused together. The leaves are alternate, linear, and 1-3 inches long. This wildflower can spread by means of underground stems.

GENTIAN

Mountain Gentian, Blue Gentian, or Parry Gentian has deep blue, upright, bell-shaped flowers. Several blossoms with light green bases grow from a single stem. There are 5 petals and sepals on each blossom which spread into 5 pointed lobes.

A less common variety is the Fringed Gentian which is also deep blue but consists of a single blossom on a stem. There are 4 fringed petals which are rounded and the tubular throat is light in color.

Gentian blooms in late summer (late August or early September) and is often found in rocky outcrops and in mountain meadows, especially in open sunlight. These flowers at times will close rapidly when it becomes cloudy.

Extracts of various species of gentian have been used for centuries for medicinal purposes, most commonly as a tonic and digestive stimulant. During the 19th century a bitter soft drink was made from the root and given the name "Beverage Moxie Nerve Food". According to the label, it was touted as a treatment for "brain and nervous exhaustion, loss of manhood, helplessness, imbecility, and insanity".

HAREBELL

This is one of the most common of the mountain wildflowers and is also known as Mountain Harebell, Bellflower, Scottish Bluebell, and Witches' Thimble. The flowers are blue-violet, bell-shaped, hang downward from a single stem, and are much larger than Chimingbells with which they are sometimes confused. The Harebell grows in dry, open areas--hillsides, valleys, clearings, and meadows. It is very abundant and blooms throughout the summer, appearing in June and often lasting until late September.

Similar flowers grow abundantly in Scotland where they have been called the "bluebells of Scotland".

IRIS

Family - Iris Family
Botanical name - *Iris missouriensis*
Season - May to July

Description -
The Rocky Mountain iris grows 1-3 feet tall with a solitary stem which is topped with a blue flower about 3 inches across. There are 3 upright petals and 3 spreading, orange-streaked sepals. The leaves are basal, pointed, nearly as tall as the stem, and sheath the stem at its base.

JACOB'S LADDER

Family - Phlox Family
Botanical name - *Polemonium*
Season - June to August

Description -
The plant is 5-10 inches high and the small flowers are 1/2 inch wide, consisting of the 5 pointed, bluish petals and 5 long stamens. In the center of the petal arrangement is a yellow throat. Leaves are basal, pinnate, with 30-40 narrow leaflets arranged so as to resemble a ladder. These can sometimes be confused with fern leaves.

IRIS

The Rocky Mountain Iris is easily recognized since it resembles the popular garden variety grown around many homes. Other common names are Blue Flag and Fleur-de-lis. The name of iris comes from the Greek and means "rainbow". This flower has been found to be depicted on an Egyptian temple dating as far back as 1450 B.C. Early Greeks planted it on the graves of women in the belief that this would lead their souls to the Elysian Fields.

The fleur-de-lis has long been associated with the French crown and the banner of Charlemagne contained a golden fleur-de-lis. It appeared on the seals of Louis VI and Louis VII. As an emblem of royalty the three parts of the flower represent wisdom, faith, and courage.

The iris blooms early in June in moist areas in the high mountain meadows. Its root contains the poison irisin, and extracts of the rootstock were used by Indians to fashion poison arrows.

It is the official flower of Tennessee.

JACOB'S LADDER

This is a very pretty, small, bluish-lavender wildflower which often grows in large clumps in moist, shady forests. It is also known as Blue Skunkleaf or Skunkleaf Polemonium and can be recognized by the five pointed, bluish petals with a yellow throat as well as by the many leaflets arranged along the stem in a ladder-like fashion. The flower generally grows above 8,000 feet and in spite of its attractive appearance, the plant has a definite skunk-like odor. Its name arises from the biblical story of Jacob and his dream of a ladder.

Native American Indians made a root tea from this plant and used it to treat pleurisy, fever, snakebite, and bowel complaints.

LARKSPUR

Family - Buttercup Family
Botanical name - *Delphinium*
Season - June to August

Description -
The stems grow 3-5 feet and at the top are 3-10 clustered flowers, dark blue to purple in color. The flower consists of 5 large sepals, one of which protrudes backward, and 4 tiny petals of which the upper pair are fringed in white. Leaves are large, palmate, and toothed.

LUPINE

Family - Legume Family
Botanical name - *Lupinus*
Season - June to August

Description -
The plant is 1-2 feet high with alternate leaves consisting of 5 leaflets joined together on a long stem (palmate). The small 1/2 inch bluish flowers are densely clustered along the upper few inches of the stem in the form of a spike. They have 5 petals and can be blue to almost white.

LARKSPUR

Larkspur is a tall, striking wildflower consisting of several navy-blue blossoms sitting near the top of a 3-4 foot stem. It has 5 large sepals one of which extends backward to form what appears to be a bird's spur (hence the name). Larkspur is common in moist areas and in aspen groves, especially close to streams.

The plant contains a poison, delphinine, which is quite toxic to cattle and if consumed in quantity can cause significant loss of stock. Surprisingly, it is non-toxic to sheep. Elk avoid eating the plant in spring but feed on it in late summer, indicating that as the plant matures it loses some of its toxicity. In earlier times, the plant was dried and made into a powder which was an effective insecticide. Native American Indians produced a blue dye from the flowers.

LUPINE

Lupine bears a great resemblance to the Texas bluebonnet, to which it is closely related. However, the mountain variety is lighter blue than its prairie cousin. In addition to the name Bluebonnet, it is sometimes called Quakerbonnet, Buffalo Clover, and Wolf Flower. There are many varieties and species but all consist of bluish, pea-like flowers clustered along a tall stem in the form of a spike. The word lupine comes from the Latin, refers to "wolf", and the name is sometimes thought to be derived from the early belief (not true) that the flower robbed the soil of nutrients and therefore was a robber or scavenger.

There are several Native American Indian legends about the lupine and its origin. The Texas bluebonnet story tells of a time when the Indian people had suffered through flood, then drought, and a severe winter. They appealed to the Great Spirit and were told that they must make a burnt offering of their most prized possession and scatter the ashes. A young girl heard of this and decided to make an offering of her most cherished doll, which had a deerskin robe and a headdress made from the bright blue feathers of a Blue Jay. Rising late at night, she built a fire, asked the Great Spirit to accept her gift and burned the doll. Afterwards she went through the fields scattering the ashes. The following morning the land was covered with beautiful blue flowers.

MONKSHOOD

Family - Buttercup Family
Botanical name - *Aconitum*
Season - June to August

Description -
 The plant is several feet tall, up to 6 feet. The flower consists of 5 purple to blue sepals with tiny, insignificant petals. One sepal covers the flower to form the hood and at the bottom is a hole to provide an entryway for insects. The leaves are broad, palmate, deeply divided, and toothed.

TALL ONE-SIDED PENSTEMON

Family - Figwort Family
Botanical name - *Penstemon*
Season - June to July

Description -
 The stem is 20-40 inches high with many blue to purple flowers arranged on only one side. The flowers are small, 3/4 inch across, and consist of 5 petals and 5 stamens. There are two upper petals which form an upper lip with a three lobed lower lip. Leaves are opposite, lance-shaped, and smooth.

MONKSHOOD

Monkshood is also called Friar's-cap or Blueweed and consists of a tall, dark purple to blue flower that has a very distinct 'hood' shape. The plant may grow up to 6 feet with the flowers near the top of the long slender stem. Of the 5 sepals, one grows over the flower in the form of a helmet which gives the characteristic appearance. Monkshood is both similar to and related to the Larkspur, but identification is easy because of the distinct appearance of each of the flowers (monkshood has the hooded shape and larkspur has the typical backward spur). The Monkshood grows in moist areas and wet meadows, oftentimes alongside streams.

All species contain a poisonous alkaloid (aconitine) which can be fatal to livestock as well as humans. The ancient Greeks and Romans used the juice from this plant to poison their arrows. There are ancient stories about monkshood, one of which relates that wearing a sprig around the neck will provide protection against werewolves.

TALL ONE-SIDED PENSTEMON

The penstemon is a very abundant mountain wildflower and has over two hundred varieties and species. We have chosen to illustrate two of the most common forms, the Tall One-sided and the Red or Southwestern Penstemon (see page 55). These are not only very common but also have a distinctive appearance and are easily identified. The tall one-sided penstemon is readily recognized by the arrangement of flowers on only one side of the stem. The color may vary from almost white to violet to dark bluish purple and the plant reaches two to three feet.

Penstemon means five stamens and there are four regular fertile stamens growing in the tubular flower and a fifth one that is elongated and hairy (this has led to the common name of Beard Tongue). The wildflower grows in open pastures and along roadsides.

A tea extract of the plant was used by Indians for a variety of medicinal purposes: for skin ailments, as an eyewash, and for stomach pain.

PINK FLOWERS
Including light purple flowers

ASPEN DAISY

Family - Composite Family
Botanical name - *Erigeron*
Season - June to August

Description -

The plant may grow over 12 inches high and the flower is small, often less than 1 inch across. The flat yellow disc head is surrounded by very many (there may be over two hundred) slender violet rays. The leaves are long, lance-like, smooth, and are alternate.

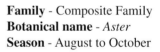

ASTER

Family - Composite Family
Botanical name - *Aster*
Season - August to October

Description -

The plant grows to 1-3 feet and there are many bright lavender and violet rays surrounding a yellow disc. The flower is 1 to 1 and 1/2 inches wide, containing broader and fewer petals than the fleabane. Leaves are long, linear and clasp the stem.

ASPEN DAISY

There are several varieties of daisies but we have selected two of the most common forms, Aspen Daisies and Ox-eye Daisies (page 73).

The Aspen Daisy, also known as Showy Daisy or Fleabane, is a very common early wildflower which can cover the meadows. The flower is small, varies from white to pale pink to lavender, and consists of many very slender rays or petals arranged around a yellow central disc.

The name of daisy comes from the Anglo-Saxon and is derived from "day's eye" which refers to the flower's closing in the evening and opening in the morning. Native American Indians are said to have applied crushed blooms of this flower to dogs to rid them of fleas, hence the name of flea-bane. Early settlers hung blossoms in their homes to keep out insects and extracts of the flower were used to treat sore throats and stomach ailments.

This flower is found almost everywhere, especially in open meadows, along roadsides, and in open aspen groves.

ASTER

Asters are the common fall wildflowers and their distinct lavender color in the meadows and along roadsides marks the prelude to coming winter. This flower is also known as Starflower or Fall Aster; the Tansy Aster is sometimes called the New Mexico Aster. These wildflowers are sometimes confused with the aspen daisy or fleabane, but can be distinguished by their blooming in late summer and early fall, their larger size, darker pink to purple color, and the larger but more sparse petals.

The word "aster" is from Latin and means "star". There is a legend about Astrea, the star maiden, who was the goddess of innocence and purity. At the time when the people of the world became violent and greedy, the gods and goddesses slowly departed the earth. The last to leave was Astrea who went up into the sky to become the constellation Virgo. Showing her compassion for the earth, she wept and her tears fell to earth as stardust and became star flowers.

Romans often placed wreaths of asters on altars and the Greeks burned the leaves to drive away evil spirits.

CLEMATIS

Family - Buttercup Family
Botanical name - *Clematis*
Season - May to July

Description -
   The vine grows along the ground or among low shrubs and trees. Flowers are about 2 inches, hang downward, are pale pink to bluish lavender, and consist of 4 sepals (no petals). Leaves are opposite, compound, with 3 oval leaflets 1-2 inches long.

CLOVER

Family - Pea Family
Botanical name - *Trifolium*
Season - June to August

Description -
   The plant grows to about 1 foot in height and the dense white to pink to red flower head is at the top of the stem and measures about 1 inch across. The leaves are compound with the 3 characteristic leaflets.

CLEMATIS

The Rocky Mountain Clematis is actually a climbing vine which may grow up to 10 feet, sometimes along the ground but often attaching itself to shrubs or trees. The flowers are pale pink to bluish lavender, usually hang downward, and consist of four large sepals (there are no petals).

The name Clematis comes from the Greek word *klema* which means vine branch and the plant is frequently found in wooded areas where the vine twines itself among the lower limbs of trees. Seeds have a striking feathery plume and these have been used as a fire starter. North American Indians used the plant as a remedy for colds and sore throats.

The common characteristic of all vines is that when the stalk touches an object the growth on that side of the stem slows. The opposite side of the stem (away from the object) grows at a normal rate, resulting in the stalk making one or more circles around the touched object.

CLOVER

There are many varieties of clover found in the mountain regions and we have illustrated one of the more common types which grows to 9,000 feet and is found in the dry, sandy soil of open meadows. The plant is very familiar to most of us because of the characteristic three leaflets (the botanical name, *trifolium*, means three leaves). Flowers of this plant are very fragrant and thus are heavily pollinated by bees. Color varies from white to pink to red.

The roots of the plant support bacteria which fix nitrogen in the soil, and for this reason, clover is often planted by farmers to restore and enrich the soil.

Clover is one of our most celebrated plants. The Greeks used clover for garlands and the English wore the leaves for good luck and as a charm against witches. The Irish species of clover, the shamrock, is the national emblem of Ireland and the three leaves of the clover were the origin of the "club", one of the suits in a deck of cards. Clover has been praised in literature from Shakespeare to Thoreau.

Native American Indians used the plant to make a poultice to treat burns, wounds, and sores. Early settlers made a syrup from the plant which was thought to be effective against asthma, bronchitis, and whooping cough.

ELEPHANT HEAD

Family - Figwort Family
Botanical name - *Pedicularis*
Season - July to August

Description -
 The spikes of this plant may grow to 2 or 3 feet and are covered with many small, 1/2 inch flowers pink to reddish purple in color. They give the appearance of many tiny elephant heads, up and down the spike. The leaves are pinnate, lobed, and fern-like.

FAIRY SLIPPER

Family - Orchid Family
Botanical name - *Calypso*
Season - June to July

Description -
 Like all orchids, the flower contains three sepals and three petals. The pink petal at the bottom forms a spoon-like lip, is spotted, and lighter in color. The flower is bearded with bright yellow hairs. There is a single large, broad leaf which sheaths the stem. The plant is small, 4 to 8 inches tall.

ELEPHANT HEAD

This is an attractive and unique flower which is always a pleasure to discover. It is also known as Little Red Elephant, Little Pink Elephant, or Elephant Flower, and consists of a dense spike of small, pink to reddish-purple flowers, each of which bears a striking resemblance to an elephant's head. The upper petal bulges at the top then curves upward to give the appearance of the trunk while three other petals form the ears and lower lip.

These wildflowers grow at high altitude, usually above 9,000 feet, and prefer moist and marshy areas. For this reason they can frequently be found around the high mountain lakes where they are grazed by elk. One species of this flower produces a root that tastes somewhat like carrots.

FAIRY SLIPPER

The Fairy Slipper, also known as *Calypso* or Venus Slipper, is actually a tiny, dainty orchid which is found in the deep forest shade. Since its growth depends on the presence of decaying wood and fungi, look for it in the moist pine and spruce forests where there are downed logs and decaying stumps. It seems to be more common between 8,000 and 10,000 feet and is the only pink or rose-colored orchid in the area.

The name is derived from the delicate structure of this small flower, which has the appearance of a tiny slipper, appropriate for a woodland fairy. The botanical name, *Calypso*, comes from the name of the beautiful nymph in Homer's *Odyssey*.

It is produced from a bulb, one half providing a single leaf and the other half giving rise to the flower stalk. This wildflower is quite rare, so do not pick; it is virtually impossible to transplant.

FIREWEED

Family - Evening Primrose Family
Botanical name - *Epilobium*
Season - June to August

Description -
   The plant is 2-6 feet tall and the bright pink blossoms, which are 1 inch across, grow near the top of the stem. The flowers bloom from the bottom upward so that there is the appearance of seed pods below, open flowers above, and a new bud at the top of the stem. The leaves are lance shaped and 2-6 inches long. They are dark green on top and light green on the underside.

GERANIUM

Family - Geranium Family
Botanical name - *Geranium*
Season - June to October

Description -
   The plant generally is 1-2 feet in height with flowers that are 1 inch broad and consist of 5 rounded, white to lavender petals with purplish veins. The leaves are basal, 2-4 inches wide and consist of 5-7 lobes.

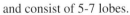

FIREWEED

Fireweed gets its name from the fact that it is one of the first flowers to appear after a forest fire. It is sometimes called Willow Weed or Blooming Sally. This rather tall, bright pink flower grows in groups or patches and is found among aspens, along streams and in disturbed soil along roadsides. The numerous seed pods produce many individual seeds, each attached to long silky hairs that act like parachutes and enable them to be widely spread by the wind. Fireweed is a favorite forage for deer, elk, and bear.

Appearing after a fire or where the soil has been greatly disturbed, this flower tends to hold the soil as well as provide food for wildlife. In addition, its brilliant pink color brightens the devastated landscape and provides hope of renewal. After the bombing raids on London during World War II, fireweed appeared among the rubble, the first to be seen since the time of Shakespeare.

The young leaves and shoots are said to be edible but should be boiled; mature leaves can be dried and used to make a tea.

GERANIUM

Wild geranium is extremely common and there are a variety of species and colors. The Wild Pink Geranium has been called Fremont Geranium, named for Charles Fremont the famous explorer of the West. There is a white geranium which is named the Richardson Geranium.

These are small whitish to light pink flowers which have 5 rounded petals with purplish veins. They can be found almost everywhere and are most common on hillsides and in open meadows; they also seem to like the aspen groves. Spreading occurs from seeds and also by thick, woody underground stems (rhizomes) which branch and produce new flower stalks at each tip. The fruit or seed pod has a long beak resembling a stork or crane bill, and this accounts for the name geranium, which comes from the Greek word for "crane".

Reddish-purple geraniums (including the Sticky Geranium and Purple Geranium) are very different in appearance from the pink ones. For this reason we have listed them separately (see page 35).

The root of this plant contains tannin, an astringent, which was once used as a styptic to stop bleeding. Extracts have also been used for gum disease, kidney disorders, and stomach ailments.

MILKWEED

Family - Milkweed Family
Botanical name - *Asclepias*
Season - June to August

Description -
    The flower head (umbel) is 2-4 inches across, is spherical, and is composed of many small, 1 inch pink and white flowers arranged in an unusual fashion. Leaves are opposite, thick, lance-shaped, and may be as long as 1 foot.

ONION

Family - Lily Family
Botanical name - *Allium*
Season - June to August

Description -
    The plant is 6-18 inches tall and the pink flower cluster (umbel) has blossoms made up of 6 small petal-like structures with protruding stamens. Leaves are basal, grass-like, narrow and smooth.

MILKWEED

Pink Milkweed or Common Milkweed, also known as Silkweed, is a large, striking flower that cannot be confused with any other plant. It grows from 2 to 6 feet in height and atop the stems are large, intricate, pink and white spherical flower heads of a unique design. It is found in fields, valleys, and along roadsides.

The plant contains very strong fibers and these can be twisted to make a crude string. Young shoots and leaves are edible but should be boiled with several changes of water to remove any bitter taste.

The botanical name, *Asclepias,* is derived from the name of the Greek god of medicine, partly because the entire plant produces a thick, milky juice which has been used for a variety of medicinal purposes. The juice has been thought to cure warts and ringworm, while an extract made from boiling the roots was used to treat dysentery, rheumatism, dropsy, tapeworm, and respiratory diseases.

In early fall, the large, banana-shaped seed pods burst open releasing many seeds, each with a silky parachute. This explains why the plant is sometimes called Silkweed.

ONION

Wild Onion or Nodding Onion is a fairly common wildflower. It is easy to recognize, consisting of pink flower clusters on the end of a long, fragile stalk which bends so that the many flowers droop downward resembling a chandelier. The protruding stamens add to the distinctive look. These plants grow in valleys or on open hillsides and the slender stem causes the flowers to "nod" in almost any breeze. The bulbs have the characteristic onion odor.

Wild onion bulbs were used, of course, by Indians and early settlers for flavoring many different foods. The young leaves can be cooked as "greens" or eaten raw in salads. Onions were also used for a variety of medicinal purposes.

PINK PLUME

Family - Rose Family
Botanical name - *Geum*
Season - June to August

Description -
The plant is 6-24 inches high and the small rounded flower has pink sepals and bracts as well as 5 pink and white petals. There are 3 flowers to a stem. The leaves are hairy, basal, fern-like and pinnately compound.

PURPLE GERANIUM

Family - Geranium Family
Botanical name - *Geranium*
Season - June to August

Description -
The plant is 1-2 feet tall and the reddish-purple flowers are 1 inch broad. There are sometimes faint white streaks on the petals and the green sepals are easily seen between the petals. Leaves are basal, 2-4 inches broad, and consist of 5-7 lobes.

PINK PLUME

The proper name of this flower is Long-plumed Avens, but Pink Plume is much more descriptive and is easier to remember. Other common names are Prairie Smoke and Old-man Whiskers. This wildflower is easily recognized by the smooth, rounded pink flowers hanging down from a stem that bends far over. There are nearly always three flowers growing from a single stem. As the flower matures and opens, the style becomes feather-like and forms the characteristic plume. These feathers, which are attached to the seeds, act as sails and cause the seeds to spread widely.

Pink plume grows in medium dry soil in meadows, on hillsides, and especially along roadsides.

Indians boiled the roots of this plant to make tea, which tastes very much like weak sassafras tea.

PURPLE GERANIUM

The most common geranium is the Pink Geranium which has already been described (see page 31). Purple Geraniums, which include the Sticky Geranium and Purple Geranium, are less abundant but are nevertheless frequently seen. They have a very different appearance and are described here.

The flower is fairly dark reddish-purple, has dark veins and faint whitish streaks on the petals. Sepals are green, elongated and are easily seen between the slightly separated petals. As the flower matures, the style elongates, often resembling a crane's bill (the name *Geranium* is derived from the Greek word for crane). Some think this stage also resembles a rocket ship, the red-tipped pistils forming the exhaust tubes.

This wildflower provides food for elk and deer.

PURPLE LOCO

Family - Pea Family
Botanical name - *Oxytropis*
Season - June to August

Description -
The plant grows 10-18 inches. Flowers are small, 1/2 to 3/4 inches, are pea-like, and arranged near the top of the stem in a spike cluster. The leaves are compound, silvery, and have silk-like hairs.

PUSSYTOES

Family - Composite Family
Botanical name - *Antennaria*
Season - June to August

Description -
Stems arise from a basal rosette of gray-green leaves and are 2-6 inches in height. The cluster heads are made up of many tiny (less than 1/8 inch across) flowers surrounded by the pink or white bracts. In fact, the flowers are so small as to be inconspicuous. Leaves are alternate, narrow, and hairy.

PURPLE LOCO

Loco is a very common flower that has many varieties, species, and colors. The easiest thing for the beginner is to regard them as either Purple Loco or White Loco. The purple variety, shown here, is actually Lambert's Loco while the white variety is shown on page 79. Purple Loco is a very showy flower and can almost cover the meadows.

This flower is also called Locoweed or Poison Vetch. Being a member of the Pea Family, the flowers are pea-like in shape, and they are bright reddish-purple, growing in dense clusters at the top of a tall stem. Purple loco generally blooms later in the season than the white variety, actually about the time that the white loco has ceased blooming.

The plant is able to extract certain minerals from the soil (in this case selenium and barium) which makes it toxic to livestock, especially horses. If the animal eats sufficient quantity, severe poisoning can bring on a disease called loco (Spanish for "crazy"). The horse may become blind, have difficulty walking, and even develop convulsions resulting in death.

PUSSYTOES

This is a small, white to pink flower that grows only a few inches in height. It is usually found in early spring (middle of June) in the dry soil of valleys, hillsides and meadows. The stems grow out of grayish-green flat leaves and contain clusters of flower heads 3/4 inches across surrounded by whitish-pink bracts. As the name implies, rubbing your finger across the flower head gives the same feel as rubbing the paw of a cat. In fact, another name for this wildflower is Catspaw.

This flower is unusual in that each plant is either all male or all female so that it produces only all male or all female flowers. In some species there are no male flowers and therefore seeds are produced without fertilization. The female flowers tend to be more pink.

It is said that a form of tobacco was made from this plant by the Navajo Indians. This was used and smoked as part of a ritual praying for rain. Also, parts of the plant were chewed in the belief this would purify the blood.

ROSE

Family - Rose Family
Botanical name - *Rosa*
Season - June to August

Description -
The bushes grow from 2 to 5 feet and are covered with many flowers that vary from delicate pink to deep rose. In the wild the flower is somewhat small, 2-3 inches across. There are 5 petals and sepals, and the leaves are pinnate and toothed.

SHOOTING STAR

Family - Primrose Family
Botanical name - *Dodecatheon*
Season - June to August

Description -
Several flowers hang from the top of a 6-16 inch leafless stalk. Each flower is 1-1 1/2 inches long, bright pink or magenta, and shaped like a dart. There is a yellow and white band near the base and the fused stamens form a black point or beak. The leaves are basal, dull green, somewhat thick, and over twice as long as they are wide.

ROSE

Wild roses are easy to recognize because they are so similar to the cultivated varieties. They have 5 delicate pink petals with many yellow stamens in the center. The stems, of course, are prickly and often reddish. The bushes grow up to 4 or 5 feet and are found in meadows, on hillsides, and along roadsides.

The rose is probably the most famous and celebrated flower in human history and was cultivated by the ancient Chinese, Egyptians, Greeks, and Romans. It was a great favorite of the Romans who wore rose garlands, bathed in rose water and strewed rose petals over floors, tables, and along paths. Some Romans stuffed their mattresses with fragrant rose petals, giving rise to the expression "a bed of roses".

The English have always had a special fondness for the rose and it is England's national flower. It has been a symbol for the English royalty as far back as the War of the Roses and its praises have been sung by many writers, from Chaucer and Shakespeare to Tennyson and Keats.

Roses were grown by both Washington and Jefferson. The famous Rose Garden at the White House was established by Mrs. Woodrow Wilson.

The small red fruit (rose hips) as well as the petals can be eaten raw or as rosebutter, rose petal jam, rose hip jam, or rose marmalade. Because of the pleasant fragrance, rose petals are used as an air freshener in the form of sachets or powders. Attar of roses is a major source of perfumes and cosmetics.

SHOOTING STAR

This is a very distinctive flower because of its magenta color, small size, and unique shape. Look for these in moist areas along the streams in late June and you may be rewarded. A closer look will reveal the resemblance to a small, brightly colored, pink dart with a black point. The petals flare backward and also give the appearance of the tail of a shooting star. These flowers often hang downward and seem to point in all directions.

Shooting stars are also known as Birdbills or American Cowslips.

THISTLE

Family - Composite Family
Botanical name - *Cirsium*
Season - June to September

Description -
   These plants grow up to 5 or 6 feet. The flower head is pink to purple, measures 1-2 inches across, and sits above sharp, stiff, green bracts. The stems are single and woolly and the leaves are long (up to 8 inches), alternate, toothed, and prickly.

VASE FLOWER

Family - Buttercup Family
Botanical name - *Clematis*
Season - May to July

Description -
   These flowers consist of four sepals (no petals), are 1 inch long and resemble an inverted urn or a bell. Color is purplish brown to lavender and the entire plant is quite hairy. Leaves are opposite, compound, finely divided, and can be up to 5 inches.

THISTLE

Thistles are familiar to many people and are usually thought of as arid or desert plants. However, several varieties live in the New Mexico mountains. Of these, Bristle Thistle is one of the most common and can be found up to 8,000 feet. It is easily noted because of its prickly leaves and large pink to purple flower heads sitting atop a long stem. It tends to attract many butterflies as well as numerous insects.

The thistle is famous in history, being mentioned in the Bible, in Greek literature, and in Teutonic legends. During the Middle Ages one form was used to treat smallpox and it was thought that wearing a piece of the plant protected one against lightning.

In spite of the spines, young leaves are quite edible, either raw (as in salads) or cooked. Boiling the leaves produces "thistle leaf tea". Herbalists recommend using an extract of the plant for treatment of heart and liver problems, fever, and infections.

VASE FLOWER

This flower's unusual shape has given rise to a variety of names: Vase Flower, Sugar Bowl, Pitcher Flower, Bell Flower, and Old Maid's Bonnet. In addition, it is sometimes called Leather Flower because of the leathery feel of the flowers.

The plant grows 1-2 feet tall and consists of dense clusters of single stems, each producing a dull reddish-lavender flower hanging like an inverted urn that has flared lips. There are no petals, only four sepals which can sometimes be purplish brown and are hairy on the outside.

Look for this flower in grasslands, meadows, and open forests. It is said that the roots are edible and tasty if flavored with vinegar and pepper; they can also be boiled and served as a sauce.

RED FLOWERS
Including orange flowers

ANEMONE

Family - Buttercup Family
Botanical name - *Anemone*
Season - June to August

Description -
   The plant is 6-12 inches high. The flowers grow on the end of a single stem, are reddish, hairy, one-half to one inch broad, and consist of sepals only. Leaves are basal, grayish, lobed, and are deeply cut into narrow segments.

CORALROOT

Family - Orchid Family
Botanical name - *Corallorhiza*
Season - June to August

Description -
   The stems grow to 20 inches, are leafless, and dark reddish brown. The small flowers, 1/2 inch across, are made up of 3 dark sepals and 3 petals, the upper 2 petals being reddish and arched over the enlarged third petal which is white with crimson spots.

ANEMONE

Anemones are widespread and there are several varieties and different colors. This is the Red Anemone (*A. globosa*) which is often found in the southern Rockies. The flowers are cup-shaped, reddish, often yellowish inside, and are hairy on the outside. They grow at the top of a single stem and are made up of sepals, there being no petals. Nearly all parts of the plant are wooly to protect it from the chilly temperatures at higher elevations (10-12,000 feet) where it is found.

Anemone comes from the Greek word *anemos* which means "wind" and this has given rise to the name of Windflower. There is a Greek legend that describes the great love of Aphrodite for Adonis and her fear that he would be hurt while hunting. When he was mortally wounded by the attack of a wild boar, she held him and wept as he died. Her tears fell and anemones grew from them.

The plant produces a bitter juice and several species contain a poison, anemonin. Native Americans made a leaf and root tea from the plant and used this for treating wounds.

CORALROOT

The Spotted Coralroot is a form of orchid, one of three represented in the book (the others are the Fairy Slipper, page 29, and the Bog Orchid, page 59). This is a most unusual plant that you are apt to miss unless you are aware of it and keep a sharp eye. It does not contain chlorophyll and thus is not green and has no leaves. Therefore, on casual glance it appears to be a reddish-brown stem without leaves which seems to be dead or dying. On close inspection, you can make out the tiny white flowers, each having a spotted tongue.

Having no chlorophyll, the plant is dependent upon living off of fungus present in decaying material. For this reason it is found in deep woods and forests where there are downed trees and decayed stumps.

The name derives from the fact that the underground stem grows in a densely interwoven pattern resembling coral. A tea made from the roots has been considered as a folk remedy for colds and fever.

FAIRY TRUMPET

Family - Phlox Family
Botanical name - *Ipomopsis* or *gilia*
Season - July to September

Description -

The stems, which are sticky, grow to 3 feet. The scarlet flowers are 1 to 2 inches long and are generally arranged along one side of the stem. Leaves are 1-2 inches long, alternate, pinnate, near the ground, and divided into narrow segments.

FIREWHEEL

Family - Composite Family
Botanical name -*Gaillardia pulchella*
Season - June to August

Description -

The plant grows 10-30 inches tall. The flower heads are 2-3 inches across and consist of a reddish-purple center or disk surrounded by many red petals with yellow tips (these tips are often toothed). The leaves are alternate and are hairy, with the lower ones being lobed while the upper leaves are narrow and tapered.

FAIRY TRUMPET

This wildflower is the Scarlet Gilia which is also called Skyrocket. The descriptive names are apt in that the flower is bright red, trumpet-shaped or rocket-shaped, with a long tubular throat that flares into 5 distinct points. It is a very common summer flower that often grows in colonies or clumps and is found in open dry areas, especially along roadsides and in meadows.

Crushing the upper leaves often produces a skunk-like odor. Navaho Indians dried the flower and produced a potion thought to be effective in treating stomach disorders.

Antelope are said to browse this plant.

FIREWHEEL

This flower goes by the names of Indian Blanket, and Sunburst as well as its proper name of Gaillardia. It is very easy to recognize with its reddish-purple center and red petals with yellow tips, altogether giving the appearance of a pinwheel. The wildflower is found in open areas, grasslands, meadows and along roadsides.

There is an American Indian legend which tells of the wife of a great chief who decided to weave a blanket for him while he was away on the warpath. She spent many hours weaving together bright colors of red, yellow and orange while her little daughter played among the folds of the blanket. One day the girl chased after a butterfly, became lost in the woods and could not find her way home. Finally, as night approached, she lay down in a clearing and asked the Great Spirit to send her the blanket which her mother had woven. The next morning she awakened to find herself covered with flowers of the same bright colors as in her father's blanket. When she was finally found by her people and showed them the beautiful flowers, they were given the name of Indian Blanket.

GLOBEMALLOW

Family - Mallow Family
Botanical name - *Sphaeralcea*
Season - June to September

Description -
   The plants grow 4-12 inches and the flowers, which are 1/2 inches broad, are orange-red or tomato-colored. The leaves are grayish green and deeply divided into 3-5 main lobes. The stamens form a tube around the pistil.

INDIAN PAINTBRUSH

Family - Figwort Family
Botanical name -*Castilleja*
Season - June to August

Description -
   Plants grow 1-2 feet in height. The tiny yellowish-green flowers are hidden by the very colorful bracts which appear to be the major part of the wildflower. Leaves are narrow, grass-like, and alternate.

GLOBEMALLOW

This flower, also known as Sore-eye Poppy or Wild Hollyhock, is found in various colors and species. The Scarlet Globemallow, shown here, is not scarlet but instead is reddish orange, actually tomato-colored. The Juniper Globemallow is a similar color, making these flowers some of the very few that are this particular shade of orange.

These globemallows are found in dry, sandy, gravelly soil among the foothills and mesas and especially among pinions and junipers. They serve as forage for deer and sheep.

Hopi Indians used this plant to treat eye ailments and gave it the name Sore-Eye Poppy. They chewed the stems like chewing gum and made an orange dye from the flowers.

INDIAN PAINTBRUSH

This flower is also called Paintbrush, Painted Cup and Squaw-feather. It is extremely common and widespread and therefore is familiar to most people. It tends to hybridize readily and thus has a variety of species and appears in many colors, such as orange, scarlet, pink, lavender, and yellow. The wildflower is noted by the fact that the color is not found in the petals of the flower, but instead in the brightly colored bracts.

This plant is partly parasitic in that its roots penetrate the roots of other plants and draw nourishment from them. It can be found almost anywhere, in open fields and meadows but also in the deep forest.

Indians used an extract of the plant to treat kidney and skin disorders and a weak tea made from the plant was thought to be effective as a love potion.

There is a Native American Indian legend which tells of a young chief who longed to be able to paint the bright colors of the sunset but had only crude paints and brushes. One evening as he watched a beautiful sunset, he heard a voice telling him to look down at the ground. There he saw a bright plant shaped like a brush and covered with paint on its tip. He used the brush and was able to transfer the paint to his picture. As he continued to paint, other brushes sprang up in various colors of the sunset. These he used, then tossed aside. The next morning, each of the discarded brushes had taken root and spread, covering the meadow with the sunset colors.

KING'S CROWN

Family - Sedum Family
Botanical name - *Sedum rosa*
Season - June to August

Description -
The plant grows from 4 to 12 inches tall and there are several thick stems. The clustered flower head is about 1 inch wide and made up of many, very tiny dark red flowers. This cluster is typically flat in appearance. Leaves are fleshy, short, alternate, and lance-shaped.

MEXICAN HAT

Family - Sunflower Family
Botanical name - *Ratibida*
Season - July to August

Description -
The plant stands 1-3 feet tall and the flowers are found on the end of a long, leafless stem. There is a tall cylindrical disk cone made up of tiny, purplish-brown disk flowers. At its base are the ray flowers, 1/2-2 inches across, and being either reddish-brown or yellow. The leaves are pinnate and 1-6 inches long; they are narrow, smooth-edged, and deeply dissected.

KING'S CROWN

King's Crown is one of several flowers that often grow in and among rocks and are therefore called stonecrop. It is also known as Roseroot and consists of a dense flat cluster of tiny dark red flowers growing at the top of a thick, fleshy stem. It is found on dry rocky slopes and often along roadcuts.

The fleshy stems and leaves are edible and can be eaten in salads.

This flower can be differentiated from a cousin, Queen's Crown, by the fact that the latter is pink and has a much more rounded head while the King's Crown is dark red with a flattened head.

MEXICAN HAT

This is actually the Prairie Coneflower but the common name of Mexican Hat is very descriptive since the flower bears a resemblance to a tall Mexican sombrero. It also goes by the name of Red Spike. The wildflower is easy to recognize because of its tall cylindrical cone of disk flowers which may be 1/2 to nearly 3 inches in length. At the base of this cone are the ray flowers (petals) which can be either reddish-brown or yellow. This is a distinctive feature of the plant--its ability to produce two different colored flowers from the same grouping of plants.

The flower is commonly found among the foothills in meadows and open areas, especially along roadsides.

North American Indians used the leaves and heads of the plant to make a form of tea.

ORANGE AGOSERIS

Family - Sunflower Family
Botanical name - *Agoseris*
Season - June to August

Description -
   The plant grows 1-2 feet. The flowers, which are at the top of a leafless stem, are 1 inch across and consist of copper-orange petals. Leaves are 2-12 inches, basal, lance-shaped, and broadest beyond the middle.

PARRY PRIMROSE

Family - Primrose Family
Botanical name - *Primula*
Season - July to August

Description -
   The plant is 1-2 feet in height and produces beautiful magenta flowers that are about 1 inch wide and contain yellow centers. Leaves are basal, forming a rosette at the base, and are long, nearly as tall as the stalk. They are 1/2 to 1 inch wide and are broadest at the tip.

ORANGE AGOSERIS

The Agoseris is known as Orange Dandlion and is a form of false dande-lion. As the name implies, it resembles the dandelion except that this flower is deep orange in color and the leaves are quite different, being lance-shaped and without prominent teeth. The flower heads are found at the top of leaf-less stems which may grow to one and one-half feet.

It tends to occur as a solitary flower and is usually seen in more dry areas, such as open meadows and along roadsides. The plant produces a milky sap which contains small amounts of rubber. Native American Indi-ans would allow this juice to gel or solidify and then chew the product as a form of chewing gum.

PARRY PRIMROSE

The Parry Primrose, also called Alpine Primrose, can grow to altitudes of 12,000 feet and when seen above timberline presents a spectacular sight. Most tundra flowers are only a few inches high, but this particular wild-flower stands 1-2 feet and consists of very beautiful magenta flowers with yellow centers. Because of its striking appearance, this wildflower is a fa-vorite of mountain climbers.

The flower is not confined to the alpine zone but also grows as low as 9,000 feet, among the forests. It is seen in marshy areas along streams and at the edges of melting snow. The brilliant color is due to certain chemicals called anthocyanins which display red color on exposure to acid conditions.

A similar flower, the Fairy Primrose, is strictly alpine (above 11,500 feet) and is only 2-4 inches high.

RED COLUMBINE

Family - Buttercup Family
Botanical name - *Aquilegia*
Season - June to July

Description -

This plant stands 10-12 inches high with the red and yellow flower on a single stem. Petals are yellow and sepals are red with long red spurs or nectar reservoirs pointing upward. The leaves are mostly basal, compound, and have rounded lobes.

RED PENSTEMON

Family - Figwort Family
Botanical name - *Penstemon*
Season - June to September

Description -
The stems grow from 2 to 4 feet high and the tubular scarlet flowers tend to hang from one side of the stem. The flowers are 1-2 inches long and have an upper and lower lip. Yellowish hairs grow at the base of the throat. The leaves are opposite, oblong and linear.

RED COLUMBINE

The Rocky Mountain Red Columbine or Comet Columbine is a cousin of the Colorado Columbine but is very different in appearance. It is bright red and yellow in color, is smaller, and usually faces downward with the long red spurs pointing upward. The flower consists of 5 yellow petals, 5 red sepals, and is about 1 inch across.

This wildflower is found in moist, shady areas so look for it in the deep forest. Its red and yellow coloring is said to attract hummingbirds which are able to reach deep into the spur and find nectar which is stored in knobs at the end. Bees and other insects also pollinate the flower but are unable to reach deep into the spur so they poke a hole in it to obtain nectar.

Although now considered somewhat poisonous, American Indians used tiny amounts of the crushed seeds to treat headache and as a love potion. A root tea was used for diarrhea and stomach trouble.

RED PENSTEMON

This penstemon, also called Scarlet Bugler or Scarlet Beard Tongue, is very common and often grows in masses. In late June and early July it begins to cover the meadows, hillsides and roadsides and is easy to spot because of the bright scarlet color. The flowers often hang on one side of the stem and are tubular in shape. They are "two-lipped" with the upper lip being 2-lobed and the lower consisting of 3 lobes. The base of the throat contains yellowish hairs (it is "bearded").

Early settlers made a syrup from boiling the flowers and this was used to treat whooping cough. Zuni Indians are said to have chewed the roots and then rubbed them on their rabbit sticks to insure a successful hunt.

WHITE FLOWERS

BANEBERRY

Family - Buttercup Family
Botanical name - *Actaea*
Season - June to July

Description -
The plant grows to 3 feet in height and the many small flowers are found in the white terminal cluster at the top of the stem. The leaves are large and basal, compound, with 3 leaflets in a maple-like appearance. The leaflets are thin and sharply toothed.

BOG ORCHID

Family - Orchid Family
Botanical name - *Habenaria*
Season - June to August

Description -
The plant grows 1-2 feet high and the flowers are arranged along the upper half of a single stem in the form of a spike. Individual flowers are 1/4 inch in length, consist of 3 petals and 3 sepals, and are fragrant. Leaves are linear, lance-shaped, and are several inches long.

BANEBERRY

Also called Snakeberry or Chinaberry, this is a shrub-like plant whose flowers are arranged in a dense cluster head that from a distance appears to be a feathery tuft of cotton. The individual flowers are quite small, white, and have 4-5 petals with prominent stamens. The wildflower is commonly found in wet and shady areas such as in deep forests near streams and springs.

After blooming, bright berries are produced which may be either red or white. The white berries are china-like in color and have a dark dot at the end (this has led to the name of "Doll's Eyes"). Both colored berries should be considered poisonous.

American Indians made a tea from the roots and used it for colds and coughs.

BOG ORCHID

This is another in the orchid family but is rather drab in appearance. Although fairly common, it is also quite inconspicuous, so you will miss it unless you look carefully. A helpful hint is found in the name, since it only grows in very wet, boggy areas, at times where there is standing water. It also goes by the name of Bog Candle or Scent Bottle and consists of a thin, waxy-white spike at the end of a single stem. The flowers which make up the spike are quite small and need to be examined closely in order to appreciate the orchid appearance. Like all orchids, the flower has 3 petals, with the lowest one (called the lip) being larger.

The roots or tubers were used for food by American Indians. It is said that if boiled for 30 minutes they taste very much like frozen potatoes.

BROOKCRESS

Family - Mustard Family
Botanical name - *Cardamine*
Season - June to August

Description -
    The plant is 1-2 feet in height and grows near water. The bright white 1/2 inch flowers are in clusters at the top of the leafy stem. The leaves are somewhat heart shaped and slightly toothed.

CALIFORNIA CORN LILY

Family - Lily Family
Botanical name - *Veratrum*
Season - July to August

Description -
    The plant grows 4-8 feet tall and has large, broad, 8-12 inch leaves. The flower head consists of long, branched, dense clusters of 1/2 inch creamy flowers, each of which has 6 petals which may be streaked with green. The leaves are striking in appearance, being broad and rounded and having heavy ribs or pleats.

BROOKCRESS

Also known as Bittercress, this wildflower consists of clusters of bright, white, 4-petaled flowers on leafy stems. It is found in very wet areas along stream banks and often seems to be growing in the water. Once you become familiar with the flower, it is very easy to recognize.

Shakespeare wrote of this flower in *Love's Labour's Lost* and described it as like "lady smocks all silver white".

Like the other cresses, this one is edible and the leaves can be added to salads. In the past, a potion made from the plant has been used to treat heart disease, epilepsy, and hysteria.

CALIFORNIA CORN LILY

This is a large, leafy plant that may be 8 feet tall and has a cornstalk-like appearance. Its most conspicuous features are the broad, yellow-green, "pleated" leaves growing along the stalk. Near the top of the plant are branched clusters of small, numerous, creamy white flowers that are streaked with green.

The plant is sometimes called False Hellebore or Skunk Cabbage and it tends to grow in patches in wet mountain meadows and along the edges of the forest. The roots are very poisonous to livestock and the flowers are poisonous to insects. A chemical within the plant is teratogenic--sheep which have eaten the plant in early pregnancy have produced lambs with deformed heads.

An extract of the plant, which contains veratrum, has been used to treat high blood pressure.

CANADA VIOLET

Family - Violet Family
Botanical name - *Viola*
Season - May to July

Description -
   The stems are 6-12 inches high and are quite thin. The white flowers are small, about 1/2 inch across and are described in the text. Leaves are heart-shaped and slightly toothed.

CHICKWEED

Family - Pink Family
Botanical name - *Cerastium*
Season - June to August

Description -
   The plant stands 4-12 inches and the flowers are 1/2 inches across. There are 5 deeply notched petals and the stamens are yellow. The leaves are narrow, opposite and about 1 inch long.

CANADA VIOLET

This variety of violet is white rather than the usual violet color one might expect. It consists of 5 white oval petals with purple veins and a yellow throat but has the characteristic "violet" shape. The two upper petals are widely separated, the two middle ones are horizontal, and the lower petal (which forms a lip) is larger and slightly triangular in shape. The lower 3 petals have purple spots and all petals are purple-tinted on the back. The lowest petal extends backward and near the base is a small sac containing the nectar.

Violets have been famous in history and literature and have long been associated with love. The white violet is representative of innocence while the blue violet is a symbol of faithful love. Surprisingly, the violet became a symbol of Napoleon Bonaparte and he presented a bouquet of violets to Josephine each year on their wedding anniversary. This flower was the symbol of the Empire until the Battle of Waterloo. Centuries earlier, the violet was the official flower of ancient Athens, the "city of the Violet Crown".

Both the flowers and leaves are edible and contain a high concentration of Vitamin C. The leaves can be boiled and eaten like spinach and the flowers have been used to make jams and jellies.

CHICKWEED

Mouse-ear Chickweed or Meadow Chickweed is a small white flower that stands only a few inches high and it is very abundant. There are 5 petals but each is deeply notched so that a casual glance suggests there are 10 petals. This notching or splitting of the petals is what gives it the "mouse ear" appearance.

The wildflower grows in meadows or open clearings, frequently in patches. Some people consider it a nuisance weed because of its tendency to invade lawns.

A tea made from this plant has long been used as an expectorant and has been applied externally for various skin disorders.

COW PARSNIP

Family - Parsley Family
Botanical name - *Heracleum*
Season - June to August

Description -
The plant grows to 4-8 feet and has large stems. The broad, flat flower cluster is 6-12 inches across and contains many tiny flowers. It is in the form of an umbel (like an umbrella), meaning all of the stems radiate from a single point. Leaves are very large and are compound, consisting of 3 lobed, toothed leaflets.

DEATH CAMAS

Family - Lily Family
Botanical name - *Zigadenus*
Season - June to August

Description -
The plant stands 8-18 inches tall with flowers grouped at the top of the stem. Each flower consists of 6 broad petal-like segments (tepals) which are cream to greenish-white in color and the stamens are as long as the segments. Characteristic are the green-colored gland spots at the base of each segment. Leaves are basal, long, grass-like, and tend to be bluish-green.

COW PARSNIP

Also known as Cow-cabbage or Masterwort, this flower is quite common and easy to recognize. It is tall, growing up to 8 feet, and the stems are topped with a large 6-12 inch flower cluster (umbel) which is very flat. The individual flowers which make up this cluster are tiny and white. This wildflower is usually found in wet areas, especially along streams.

The Indians are said to have used this plant for food, including the leaves, peeled stems and roots (however one should be careful about eating this plant unless careful identification is made since some species are poisonous). It still serves as forage for wild and domestic animals, especially elk. Root tea was thought by the Indians to be helpful for colic, cramps, headache, sore throat, and flu.

The botanical name *Heracleum* arises from the name of Hercules, the mythological symbol of great strength.

DEATH CAMAS

You should try to discover and identify this flower if for no other reason than its rather ominous name. It tends to grow in moist, cool places such as open forests and consists of creamy or greenish-white flowers grouped near the top of a straight slender stem. There are 6 petal-like segments (called tepals) and the flower's distinguishing feature are the green spots or glands at the base of each segment.

As the name implies, it is highly poisonous because of a toxic agent, zygadenim, which is found in all parts of the plant. Livestock, especially sheep, have died as a result of grazing the flower and there have been deaths of humans who have eaten parts of the plant. It has an onion-like bulb which on rare occasion has been mistaken for the bulb of an edible lily and when eaten, has led to disastrous results.

EVENING PRIMROSE

Family - Evening Primrose Family
Botanical name - *Oenothera*
Season - June to August

Description -
   The plant grows 3-10 inches and the flowers seem very close to the ground. There are 4 white petals with long yellow stamens, the entire flower being 3-4 inches across. Leaves are pinnate and seem to cluster near the ground.

FALSE SOLOMON SEAL

Family - Lily Family
Botanical name - *Smilacina*
Season - June to August

Description -
   The plants reach 2-3 feet in height. Flower clusters are 2-4 inches long and are made up of very tiny (1/10 inch) white flowers having 3 petals and 3 sepals. Leaves are large, 3-8 inches long, ovate and clasp the stem. There is a thick, horizontal root.

EVENING PRIMROSE

Evening Primrose or Sandlily is easy to recognize. It is a large white flower with 4 thin petals, yellow stamens, and grows close to the ground. The petals turn pink with age and begin to wither, so that in any group of these white flowers there are a few scattered pink ones. The plant grows best in dry soil and likes disturbed areas so is often seen on roadside slopes.

As its name implies, this flower first opens in the evening, remains open through the night, and may be partially open the following day. It releases a very strong fragrance which attracts night-flying insects, especially moths.

The Yellow Evening Primrose is a very different flower so it is described separately (see page 105).

FALSE SOLOMON SEAL

This wildflower is a lily-like plant consisting of leafy stems ending in a dense, elongated cluster of very tiny white flowers. Also called Solomon-plume, this flower should be differentiated from the True Solomon Seal whose small flowers are star-shaped. The plant tends to grow in cool, shady, moist areas in the forest and is often found in dense patches. After flowering, red berries with purplish dots are produced which are edible though slightly bitter (be careful these are not confused with Baneberry whose red berries are poisonous).

There are several theories as to how this flower got its unusual name. One interesting idea, referring to the True Solomon Seal which has star-shaped flowers, relates that if one dips the flower in ink and applies it to paper, an image is produced of the Star of David (also known as the Seal of Solomon).

Indians made a tea from the roots, supposedly useful for rheumatism, stomach disorders, as a blood purifier, and as a "female tonic".

GRASS-OF-PARNASSUS

Family - Saxifrage Family
Botanical name - *Parnassia*
Season - July to September

Description -
The plant grows to 2 feet with slender, unbranched stems. Flowers are 1 inch across, have 5 white, star-shaped petals which are clearly fringed at the base, and there are yellow, fan-shaped structures between the stamens. Leaves are basal, stalked, and heart-shaped except for a single, small leaf half way up the stem.

GREEN GENTIAN

Family - Gentian Family
Botanical name - *Swertia*
Season - June to August

Description -
The tall thick stem grows from 4 to 6 feet and has large, 1 foot leaves that are broad at the base and smaller near the top. These are arranged in whorls consisting of 4-6 leaves. The flowers are small, 1/2 to 3/4 inches broad, and grow close to the stem. There are 4 petals, greenish-white with purple spots.

GRASS-OF-PARNASSUS

This rather strange sounding name refers not to a grass, but to a pretty white flower with distinctive petals. Other names are Rocky Mountain Parnassia and Fringed Parnassia. The flowers are about 1 inch across, are saucer-shaped, and have 5 petals. The distinguishing features are the petals which are clearly fringed at their base, and the yellow fan-shaped structures between the stamens. Another interesting characteristic is the fact that although the leaves grow from the base (they are basal), there is always a single small leaf half way up the stem.

Parnassus is the name of a mountain in Greece that was thought by the ancients to be the home of the Muses. It is assumed that this flower grew there in large numbers, hence the name.

GREEN GENTIAN

At first glance, this plant does not appear to be a wildflower at all, but instead, a tall (up to 7 feet) green stalk with large leaves arranged in whorls, presenting an almost cornstalk-like appearance. Close inspection will reveal that growing along the stem are many small greenish-white flowers showing purple spots and having an unusual appearance.

This plant also goes by the names of Deer-ears, Monument Plant, and Elkweed. Because of its size it is very conspicuous and can be spotted from a distance. It tends to grow in open pine forests and aspen groves.

Indians ground the roots to powder, added a small amount to water and applied the mixture to the skin in hopes of controlling fever. Even though the root is said to be a mild laxative, Apaches used it for food.

MARIPOSA LILY

Family - Lily Family
Botanical name - *Calochortus*
Season - July to August

Description -
   The plant grows 8-20 inches and there is a single flower at the top of the stem. There are 3 broad white petals, 3 narrow green sepals, and 6 prominent yellow stamens. The flower is 2-3 inches wide and there is a purple band or spot at the base of the petals. Leaves are long, linear, and grass-like.

MARSH MARIGOLD

Family - Buttercup Family
Botanical name - *Caltha*
Season - June to August

Description -
   The plant is 4-8 inches high. The bowl shaped flower consists of 5-15 narrowly oval sepals which are white and sometimes blue-tinged. Each flower is 1-2 inches across and the yellow center is formed by many yellow stamens. Leaves are basal, oval or rounded, and light green. The stems are purplish.

MARIPOSA LILY

This is another example of a beautiful and unique flower which is easy to identify and remember. It is also known as Sego Lily and Star Tulip. The wildflower appears in the middle of July and can be found growing singly in open meadows and fields. It has a triangular or goblet-shaped appearance and consists of 3 broad white petals with a dark purple band or purple spots at the base and there are 6 conspicuous yellow stamens.

The word mariposa is Spanish for butterfly and the flower is aptly named. It is the official flower of Utah.

The entire plant is edible, especially the bulb or root which tastes like potato. Indians ground the roots into flour which was used to make bread.

MARSH MARIGOLD

As the name implies, this flower is found in very wet places, such as marshy meadows, soggy areas, and along stream banks. It can even grow in water. Other names by which it is known are Meadowbright and White Marshmarigold. The plant is only a few inches high and the white flowers are solitary, growing on a leafless stem. They are bowl-shaped or buttercup-like, and consist of narrow white sepals which may be blue tinged; there are no petals. This flower appears early in spring, sometimes seemingly uncovered by melting snow.

From the root of this plant, a tea was made to which was added maple syrup and this became popular with the early settlers as a form of cough syrup. A similar extract from the plant was thought to be useful to treat snakebite.

All parts of the plant may irritate and even blister the skin.

OXEYE DAISY

Family - Sunflower Family
Botanical name - *Leucanthemum*
Season - June to September

Description -

The plant is 10-24 inches high and the 2-3 inch flower grows on a single, nearly leafless stem. The flower consists of a golden disk center surrounded by numerous white rays or petals. The leaves which form the basal rosette are spoon-shaped with toothed margins. Upper leaves are narrow with wavy, toothed margins.

SANDWORT

Family - Pink Family
Botanical name - *Arenaria*
Season - July to September

Description -

The plant reaches 4-10 inches in height. Flowers grow in clusters with many slender stems, are bright white with 5 petals, and each flower is only 1/3 inches across. The purple stamens seem to be spots on the petals. The leaves are grass-like, in tufts, and are pointed, opposite, and 1-3 inches long.

OXEYE DAISY

There are various types of daisies but the Oxeye is very common and in mid-summer can cover the meadows and be found in abundance along road-sides. It is not native but was brought to America from Europe and subsequently spread over much of the country. This is the common daisy of folk-lore which led to the saying "loves me, loves me not ...". For the person reciting this, the result is usually favorable because most all of the flowers have an uneven number of petals.

This composite with its yellow disk and bright white rays is very famil-iar and easy to recognize. It spreads easily by producing many seeds (100-300 per flower) and also propagates through underground stems called rhi-zomes.

Next to the rose, this flower is the most famous in history and literature. Daisies are mentioned in works of Chaucer, Shelly, Dante, and Dryden. Poems dedicated to the daisy were written by Wordsworth and Burns while Shakespeare used the daisy as a symbol of innocence in *Hamlet*.

In horse racing, the term "daisy cutter" is used to refer to a horse which lifts his feet only slightly while running. The same term is used in baseball to refer to a hard hit ball which barely skims the ground.

SANDWORT

Shown here is Fendler's Sandwort which is a small white flower grow-ing in clusters only a few inches high. Its identifying characteristic is the fact that the tips of the stamens are dark reddish-purple and on first glance these appear to be red spots on the petals. As its name implies, the plant grows in sandy soil and therefore is found in sunny, dry, rocky locations. The flower can be confused with Chickweed but does not have deeply notched petals.

This flower is a member of the Pink family which includes chickweed, baby's breath, dusty miller, dianthus and campion. The term wort, which simply means "plant", is frequently used in combination to describe many different flowers--figwort, milkwort, sandwort, lousewort, etc.

STRAWBERRY

Family - Rose Family
Botanical name - *Frageria*
Season - June to September

Description -
  The plant grows along the ground, is less than 8 inches in height, and has runners that are reddish in color. Flowers are small, have 5 white petals and many stamens. The compound leaves have 3 leaflets which are blue-green, broad and oblong, and are toothed on the upper part.

THIMBLEBERRY

Family - Rose Family
Botanical name - *Rubus*
Season - June to August

Description -
  This plant grows 3-5 feet in height. The flowers are 1-2 inches across, are bright white in color, and consist of 5 petals and many stamens. Leaves are large, several inches wide and are five-lobed.

STRAWBERRY

Wild Strawberry is a very common plant of the mountain forests. It is low and spreading, with reddish runners, and in May and early June produces a pretty, white, 5-petaled flower. There are three leaves which are often blue-green. In July and August the berries are produced, and these have the typical strawberry appearance, though are quite small. When ripe, they are very tasty.

Indians ate the berries and made a leaf tea which was a popular beverage. Early settlers not only ate the strawberries but also used them to make jam and jelly. Today, the berries serve as a source of food for a wide variety of wildlife, including birds, rodents, and both brown and grizzly bears.

THIMBLEBERRY

The Western Thimbleberry is sometimes called Salmonberry and is in a large group of plants named *Rubus*, which in Latin means "bramble". A cousin is the New Mexico Raspberry. The Thimbleberry plant generally grows 3-4 feet high, has white flowers growing in clusters of three or more, and has large leaves. It can be found in moist, wooded areas.

The fruit which is produced is raspberry-like and though edible, is not very tasty. Nevertheless, the fruit serves as food for birds and bears, while the plant is eaten by deer.

WHITE CAMPION

Family - Pink Family
Botanical name - *Silene*
Season - June to August

Description -
The plant is 1-3 feet in height with several stems which are covered with glandular hairs. The white flowers are 3/4 inches wide and are made up of 5 petals about 1 inch long, notched at the tip. Leaves are mostly found on the lower half of the plant, are 1-4 inches long and are smooth, opposite, and lance-like.

WHITE CHECKERMALLOW

Family - Mallow Family
Botanical name - *Sidalcea*
Season - July and August

Description -
The plant grows 1-3 feet in height, usually close to water. Flowers are clustered near the top of the stem, are about 1 inch wide, and are made up of 5 thin, delicate white petals which are somewhat squared at the tip. Stamens are fused into a long tube. The leaves are basal, palmate, and coarsely toothed.

WHITE CAMPION

There are two varieties of white campion, Bladder Campion and White Campion, which are quite similar but have slightly different petals. These flowers grow at the end of a long stem and are easily identified by the calyx (a term to mean the sepals collectively) which lies below the petals. It is large, tubular, bulbous, and almost appears to be inflated. The flowers themselves are white and have 5 petals which are notched at the tip.

On any given plant the flowers are either all male or all female. On male flowers the tubular bladder is thin and has about ten veins while the female flower shows a more bulbous calyx having about twenty veins.

The White Campion is usually found in fairly dry places such as meadows, fields, and brushy areas. It is a night bloomer which attracts moths.

WHITE CHECKERMALLOW

This wildflower is also known as Modest Mallow or Wild Hollyhock. It is very striking and consists of many delicate white flowers with 5 thin petals clustered at the top of an unbranched stalk. The fused stamens form a long tube that spreads near the tip. It can be found in moist, shady sites, especially along the streams.

Europeans made marshmallow candies from the root juice of the old-world Marsh Mallow. The root pulp was boiled to soften it, then cooled, and sugar was added, thus forming the white puffy marshmallow. Today these candies are made from gelatin which is a much cheaper ingredient.

From the common mallow the Romans produced a tea or drink which was thought to be effective against many diseases. A poultice made from the plant was used to relieve pain from swellings and insect bites.

WHITE LOCO

Family - Pea Family
Botanical name - *Oxytropis*
Season - May to July

Description -
The plant grows to 10-18 inches. Flowers are white, about 1 inch across, pea-like, and grow near the top of the stem in spike clusters. Seed pods are covered with black hairs, and when dry, rattle in the wind. The leaves are compound and tend to be silver in color.

YARROW

Family - Sunflower Family
Botanical name - *Achillea*
Season - June to October

Description -
The plant stands 2-3 feet high and the stems have small white hairs. The small white flowers have 5 rounded rays which are 1/8 inches long and have 3 teeth at the tip; the disks are yellow. These flowers grow in flat clusters of 10-30 at the top of the stem. Leaves are feathery or fern-like and are basal.

WHITE LOCO

Also known as Locoweed, Poison Vetch, and Rattleweed, this flower appears in early spring and can cover the meadows with bright white patches. Loco occurs in many varieties, but for the sake of simplicity, can be regarded as either White Loco or Purple Loco.

The flowers are pea-like and grow along the upper part of a leafless stem in clusters to form a spike. The plant is found growing in large colonies in dry areas, especially open meadows. Seed pods, when they have dried, tend to clatter in the wind, hence the name of Rattleweed.

The plant absorbs selenium from the soil and produces an alkaloid that can be poisonous to livestock, especially horses. If the animal consumes sufficient quantity, disease occurs termed "loco" (Spanish for "crazy"). The animal becomes dull, listless, unsteady in gait, and may run into objects. Rarely, the condition can prove fatal.

YARROW

Also known as Milfoil, this wildflower is very abundant, occurs throughout the summer season and has a reputation as a cure-all. As many as 10-30 tiny white flowers grow in flat-topped clusters at the end of a tough, fibrous stem. It is found in dry, open areas such as meadows and fields, and has an unpleasant odor. If cows graze the plant, their milk develops a bitter taste.

The botanical name is derived from the Greek warrior, Achilles, who is said to have treated his soldier's wounds with a poultice made from the plant. It contains an alkaloid, Achillium, which has styptic qualities and can slow bleeding. For this reason, American Indians called it the "nosebleed plant". Herbal tea made from this plant has been used to treat colds, fever, indigestion, headache, rheumatism, internal bleeding, and anorexia.

The Swedes call the plant "field hops" and have used it in making beer.

YELLOW FLOWERS

ARNICA

Family - Sunflower Family
Botanical name - *Arnica*
Season - June to August

Description -
The plant is 6-20 inches high and has single hairy stems. Flowers are 1-3 inches wide with the yellow rays being notched at the tip. Leaves are paired, opposite, and the more basal ones are heart- shaped or valentine-shaped. Upper leaves are smaller and more narrow.

BLACK-EYED SUSAN

Family - Sunflower Family
Botanical name - *Rudbeckia*
Season - June to August

Description -
Stems grow to 12-20 inches and are often purple. Flowers are yellow composites, 2-3 inches wide, and have a dark brown to black disk that is conical and bulging; petals or rays are drooping. Leaves are long, narrow, alternate, and hairy.

ARNICA

This wildflower is a pretty yellow composite found growing at the end of single, hairy stem and having 10-15 rays with notched tips. (Like all composites, it has a central disc or center surrounded by rays or petals.) In the case of the Arnica, the rays are almost the same color as the disk. There are two main types, Heartleaf Arnica and Long-leaf Arnica, whose flowers are very much alike but are distinguished by the differences in the leaves. The Heartleaf variety is shown here and has basal leaves which are paired and are heart-shaped or kidney-shaped. The Long-leaf variety has narrow or lance-shaped leaves and lacks the heart-shaped basal leaves.

Arnica grows in moist, shaded areas and is usually found in the forest. It is grazed by mule deer. Early settlers made a salve using an extract of the plant and applied this to cuts in order to keep down infection.

BLACK-EYED SUSAN

This is a Midwestern plant which has become widespread over much of the country. It resembles a sunflower except that the disk head is dark chocolate to black and is raised in the form of a bulging cone. Because of this shape of the disk, some of the flower's relatives are called coneflowers. Other distinguishing features are the petals (rays or ray flowers), which tend to droop downward and the stems, which are hairy and have fine grooves.

This flower is found in open meadows, forest clearings and grasslands. The botanical name, *Rudbeckia*, was chosen to honor Olaf Rudbeck, a noted Swedish botanist. Nurserymen have developed improved varieties which are sometimes known as glorioso daisies.

Native American Indians made a tea from the roots and used this for colds and earaches.

BRACTED LOUSEWORT

Family - Figwort Family
Botanical name - *Pedicularis bracteosa*
Season - July to September

Description -
   This tall plant produces its flowers at the upper end of a strong stem. The flowers are small, about 1 inch across, and are yellow with definite reddish markings. The upper lips are narrow and arched outward like a beak. Leaves are 3-10 inches and are fernlike.

BUTTER AND EGGS

Family - Figwort Family
Botanical name - *Linaria*
Season - July to September

Description -
   The plant is 1-3 feet with flowers growing along the upper end of a strong stem. The flowers themselves are small, about 1 inch across and are pale yellow and yellow-orange. There is an upper lip made up of 2 yellow lobes and a lower lip consisting of 3 yellow lobes showing the orange patch. The leaves are narrow, 1-4 inches long, quite numerous, and grayish-green in color.

BRACTED LOUSEWORT

There are several varieties of Lousewort but this one is easy to identify because of its large size. Descriptive names that are easier to remember are Towering Lousewort, Tall Lousewort, and Fernleaf. The plant is 3-5 feet tall with flowers arranged near the top in the form of a spike and the individual flowers are small, yellow with reddish markings, and beak-like in appearance. This wildflower is usually found in moist woods and meadows. Its thick stem allows it to withstand the strong winds at high altitude.

Green shoots and the flowering heads of the plant are eaten by elk. Native American Indians concocted a root tea which was used for stomach pain, anemia, heart trouble and as a cough medicine.

BUTTER AND EGGS

This flower, which appears in mid-summer, is easy to identify and remember because of its unique coloring and its unforgettable name. The plant is about 1-3 feet tall with the small flowers arranged near the top of the stem in the form of a spike. The flowers themselves are snapdragon-like in appearance and are two-toned, one shade being the color of butter and the other the color of egg yolk. Each flower has two upper lobes and three lower lobes, the lower ones containing the bright yellow-orange patch.

The wildflower grows commonly in sunny areas such as meadows and along roadsides, especially in disturbed soil. It can spread by means of underground stems (rhizomes) which accounts for the fact that it often appears in patches. There is a long spur at the base of the flower which contains nectar. If this is held up to the light you may be able to see the level of the nectar within the spur.

A leaf tea made from the plant has been used as a laxative as well as for the treatment of dropsy, jaundice, and skin diseases. In early times the flowers served as a source of yellow dye.

There is an old adage that if you walk three times around a patch of butter and eggs this will break any spell which has been cast upon you.

BUTTERWEED

Family - Sunflower Family
Botanical name - *Senecio*
Season - May to August

Description -

The shrubby or bushy plant grows to 2-3 feet. Flowers are small (1/2 inch) and arranged in terminal clusters with the golden rays appearing separate and uneven. Stems are purple. The leaves are toothed and somewhat deeply cut, are larger at the base becoming smaller above.

CINQUEFOIL

Family - Rose Family
Botanical name - *Potentilla*
Season - June to October

Description -

The Bush Cinquefoil is 1-4 feet in height while the Leafy Cinquefoil is 6-12 inches tall. There are 5 broad, rounded, yellow petals and 5 sepals; the individual flowers are about 1 inch across. Leaves are pinnately compound with 3-7 (usually 5) leaflets and the leaves of the Leafy variety are basal.

BUTTERWEED

Also known as Golden Ragwort, this flower belongs to a very large group of plants named *Senecio* and in this group are many different varieties which are difficult to differentiate. For the sake of simplicity, we have illustrated two varieties that are both common and easy to identify: the Butterweed (shown here) and the Nodding Groundsel (see page 97).

This is a bushy plant with small composite flowers growing in terminal clusters. The individual flowers have yellow rays (petals) which are separated, unevenly spaced, and appear disorganized. Look for it in dry areas, especially along roadsides and on gravelly slopes.

This plant contains a toxic alkaloid and is potentially poisonous to livestock if consumed in sufficient quantity.

CINQUEFOIL

In mountainous areas, the name Cinquefoil usually refers to a shrub or bush that is very abundant and seems to grow everywhere (Bush Cinquefoil or Shrubby Cinquefoil). It produces a bright yellow flower that blooms throughout the summer and provides a background of color in the fields and meadows, along the streams, and even in the open forest. With its flowers of 5 rounded yellow petals and its reddish-brown bark, this bush is readily recognized and not easily confused with any other plant.

There is also a Cinquefoil flower, Leafy Cinquefoil (not illustrated here), which blooms in mid-summer and produces an almost identical yellow flower with 5 rounded petals. The leaves of the Leafy Cinquefoil are generally basal.

The term cinquefoil means "five leaves" and although there are not always this exact number of leaflets, this is the most common number. The shrub retains its leaves in winter and provides forage for a variety of wildlife.

DANDELION

Family - Sunflower Family
Botanical name - *Taraxacum*
Season - May to October

Description -
The bright yellow flower head, 1 to 1 1/2 inches broad, grows at the top of a single hollow stem that stands 2-12 inches high. Leaves are basal, vary in length from 2 to 16 inches long, are lance-shaped, and have very jagged teeth.

GLOBEFLOWER

Family - Sunflower Family
Botanical name - *Trollius*
Season - May to July

Description -
The plant is 10 to 18 inches in height with yellowish or cream-colored flowers 1 to 1 1/2 inches wide. There are 5-7 sepals (no petals) and many yellow stamens. Leaves are palmate, 5-lobed, jagged, and toothed.

DANDELION

This very familiar plant is also known as Blowball, Puffball, and Golden Tramp. To many homeowners and gardeners it is regarded as a disagreeable and pesky weed, but in early spring it produces a striking golden flower which can fill the meadows with the first bright patches of color. The single yellow flower head sits atop a hollow stem which arises from the center of a rosette of toothed leaves. There is a long, tough tap root which can continue to grow even if cut, so that eradication of the plant is difficult.

The name dandelion comes from the French words *dent-de-lion* which means "lion's teeth" and refers to the jagged toothed leaves.

Children have always enjoyed this plant, learning to blow the puffballs and remembering the old adage that if one can blow away all the seed heads with a single breath, a wish will be granted. They also quickly discover that the hollow stems are excellent for blowing bubbles.

Both the leaves and roots are edible and can be added to salads and soups. Dandelion wine is made from the fermented flower heads and a root tea has been used for liver and kidney ailments. Today, the plant serves as a major source of food for a variety of wildlife--birds, deer, elk, and bear.

GLOBEFLOWER

This flower is sometimes confused with the Marsh Marigold since both of them tend to grow in similar, wet habitats: bogs, marshes, and near melting snow. In early summer as the snows recede from the high mountain meadows, both flowers can often be found growing together. Careful examination reveals the globeflower to be yellowish or creamy-colored while the marsh marigold is distinctly white. In the field view shown here there are a number of globeflowers with one or two bright white marigolds. Another means of easy identification is the marked difference in the leaves, the globeflower having lobed, toothed leaves while the marigold's are rounded.

Each globeflower is bowl-shaped, grows from a single stem, and consists of 5-7 cream-colored sepals (there are no petals). There are many prominent yellow stamens.

GOLDENROD

Family - Sunflower Family
Botanical name - *Solidago*
Season - July to September

Description -
 The large variety is usually 2-5 feet in height. The individual flowers are about 1/8 inch across and are arranged in long, rather flat-topped clusters along one side of the curved branches. Leaves are 2-5 inches long, are lance-shaped, alternate, and have 3 prominent veins.

GOLDEN SMOKE

Family - Fumitory Family
Botanical name - *Corydalis*
Season - June to September

Description -
 The bush-like plant grows 6-24 inches in height. Flowers grow in loose clusters, are yellow, and about 3/4 inches long. The 4 petals, all quite different, combine to give a tubular appearance. Leaves are 3-6 inches long and are soft, pinnate, blue-green, and fern-like.

GOLDENROD

Goldenrod is common throughout the United States, is familiar to many people, and the mountain variety, Meadow Goldenrod or Yellowweed, is similar to the flower found elsewhere. It is a large plant, up to 5 feet in height, and topped with tiny yellow flowers clustered in curving plumes. The flowers usually grow on only one side of the curved branches.

There is also a smaller variety (also shown here) which is only 1-2 feet high with the small flower heads growing more in rounded clusters. This form tends to appear slightly later in the season than the large one. Both varieties grow in meadows and open woodlands up to an altitude of 8,500 feet.

In the past hayfever was thought to be caused by this plant until it was discovered that the actual culprit is ragweed (Goldenrod pollen is not spread by the wind, only by insects). Goldenrod was used by American Indians for a variety of medicinal purposes: skin ulcers, boils, colds and rheumatism. The roots were chewed in an effort to relieve toothache.

The plant contains latex from which Thomas Edison attempted to produce a commercial form of rubber. In fact, at one time Henry Ford made a single set of goldenrod tires (they were terribly expensive).

GOLDEN SMOKE

This wildflower with its unusual name consists of a bushy plant containing loose clusters of tubular yellow flowers having weak stems. There are only 4 petals, all different, which combine to produce the tubular effect. The upper petal has an arched hood in front and a rounded hollow spur behind while the lower spur forms a scoop in front. The side petals face one another and form a tube containing the stamens.

This flower commonly occurs in disturbed soil and especially on rocky, sandy hillsides.

GROMWELL

Family - Borage Family
Botanical name - *Lithospermum*
Season - June to September

Description -
 The plant is 1-3 feet high and has many stems. The yellow flowers are about 1 inch long and are funnel-shaped, growing in clusters which bend from the top of the stem. Leaves are long, narrow, grayish, and clasp the stem. Both the leaves and stems are hairy.

HOLLYGRAPE

Family - Barberry Family
Botanical name - *Mahonia*
Season - May to July

Description -
 The plant is only a few inches high and grows along the ground. Flowers are small, in clusters, and contain 6 yellow petals and 6 sepals. Leaves are compound with 3-7 leaflets, are leathery, and spiny-toothed. They are evergreen, often turning red in fall and winter.

GROMWELL

This wildflower is also known as Manyflower Gromwell and Manyflower Puccoon. It is a bushy plant with many stems and has bright yellow or yellow-orange flowers that are funnel-shaped. These grow in coiled clusters that bend from the top of a hairy stem.

The flower tends to grow in rocky or gravelly soil on banks and hillsides and is often found in open pine forests. An extract of the plant was used for a variety of medical purposes and the roots are edible. Native American Indians used the root to produce a purple dye.

The seeds produced by this plant are pearly white and very hard. This accounts for the botanical name of *Lithospermum* which means stone seed. The French call this flower *"plante aux perles"* because of the resemblance of the seeds to pearls.

HOLLYGRAPE

Hollygrape is neither holly nor grape but gets its name from its holly-like leaves and the dark blue berries. Also known as Creeping Hollygrape, Barberry, and Mountain Holly, it is closely related to Oregon Grape, the state flower of Oregon. The plant is very low-growing, spreads by underground stems, and appears as a form of groundcover. In spring it produces clusters of small, bright yellow flowers which are replaced in late summer by the dark bluish berries. The leaves last through winter but in the fall many of them turn red and brighten the landscape.

The berries can be eaten raw but are rather sour. If sweetened with sugar, a drink can be made that is similar to grape juice, and the berries have long served as a source of jellies and jams. They are still a major food source for a variety of wildlife.

North American Indians made a yellow dye from the roots of this plant and also made a root tea which was used as a tonic.

MONKEYFLOWER

Family - Figwort Family
Botanical name - *Mimulus*
Season - June to September

Description -
   The bushy-like plant is 6-24 inches in height and grows in very wet soil. The flowers are 1 to 1 1/2 inches broad with 2 upper and 3 lower lobes. Red spots at the throat attract and guide insects. Leaves are 1-4 inches, opposite, oval, and toothed.

MULLEIN

Family - Figwort Family
Botanical name - *Verbascum*
Season - June to September

Description -
   The stems are strong and woody. Flowers are small, 3/4 inches broad, have 5 symmetrical yellow petals, and grow in a tightly packed spike near the top of the stalk. Leaves tend to be basal, are 4-16 inches long, whitish, and covered with woolly hairs giving a velvet feel and appearance.

MONKEYFLOWER

Yellow Monkeyflower is an interesting yellow flower that grows in very wet areas such as stream banks, marshes, and around springs and lakes. As the name implies, the flower at times has the appearance of a monkey's face. There are 2 upper lobes bent upward, 3 lower lobes bent downward, and the red spots produce the face-like or mask-like effect (the botanical name *Mimulus* means "mask").

The leaves are edible and have been eaten in salads, giving rise to the common name of Wild Lettuce.

MULLEIN

This is an unusual plant which many people will recognize, but do not know its name. Mullein goes by a variety of common terms: Woolly Mullein, Blanketweed, Torchweed, Miner's Candle, Witch's Candle, and Candelaria. The plant often grows in colonies and resembles a tall (up to 7 feet) pole with small yellow, densely packed flowers in a spike near the top. The entire plant is covered with a mat of woolly hairs giving the leaves a velvety feel. It is found in dry soil in open meadows and especially along roadsides. In winter the dead brown stalks remain standing and often appear above the snow (they can remain in place for up to 3 years).

Early Greeks and Romans dipped the stalks in tallow to make torches and used parts of the stalk as lamp wicks. In North America the early Spaniards dried the leaves, wrapped them in corn husks, and produced cigarettes. These "mullein cigarettes" were thought by the settlers to be beneficial in treating asthma.

The soft leaves were used as shoe liners and an oil extracted from the leaves was employed as a remedy in treating earache. Frontier women would rub their cheeks with the leaves to produce a rosy glow, giving rise to the name of "Quaker's rouge".

NODDING GROUNDSEL

Family - Sunflower Family
Botanical name - *Senecio*
Season - July to September

Description -
The plant grows 1-3 feet in height and has leafy stems. Yellow flower heads growing on individual stalks are 1/2 inch broad and 3/4 inch long; they turn downward or droop. Bracts are all the same length and are frequently purple. The leaves are 4-8 inches long, lance-like, toothed, and are sheathed on the stem.

PARRY LOUSEWORT

Family - Figwort Family
Botanical name - *Pedicularis*
Season - June to August

Description -
The plant grows 4-12 inches high. Flowers are small, creamy or yellow, tube-shaped, with the upper lip forming a beak. The leaves are pinnate, fern-like, long, and narrow.

NODDING GROUNDSEL

This wildflower belongs to a large group of plants known as *Senecio* that contains many forms and varieties. We have included two of the members of this group that are easy to identify, the flower shown here plus Butterweed (see page 87).

Nodding Groundsel is recognized by its half-inch drooping yellow flower heads that do not contain petals. In addition, its easily visible bracts are often purplish. The flower is usually found in the fairly moist soil of meadows, fields, and open forests.

Some of these plants can be poisonous to livestock, but fortunately, they are seldom eaten in much quantity.

PARRY LOUSEWORT

This flower is another in the group of Louseworts that is fairly easy to identify (see Bracted Lousewort, page 85). The plant is only a few inches tall and the small yellow flowers have a beak-like appearance. The flowers are arranged around the plant in a circular or whorled fashion and, when viewed from above, it is apparent that the flowers nearly always point in a clockwise direction. This results in a very striking pin-wheel effect.

The wildflower is found in medium-moist soil in open woodlands, especially pine forests.

Early American settlers would rub the flowers into their children's hair in the belief that this would get rid of head lice, thus the name of lousewort.

PARSLEY

Family - Parsley Family
Botanical name - *Pseudocymopterus*
Season - June to September

Description -
  Plants are 1-2 feet in height. The individual, tiny yellow flowers grow in a flat-topped compound umbel. Leaves are narrow, pinnately compound, parsley-like and sheathed on the stems.

SALSIFY

Family - Sunflower Family
Botanical name - *Tragopogon*
Season - June to September

Description -
  The plant grows 1-3 feet high and produces a single flower on a hollow stem. Flowers are 1-2 inches across, have yellow petals and the bracts are very long, extending beyond the petals. Leaves are 5-6 inches long, thin, and grass-like.

PARSLEY

Wild Parsley or Mountain Parsley is a relative of the common parsley found in food stores. It is a member of a family of plants which includes carrots, celery, fennel, coriander, cumin, dill, and anise. Mountain Parsley has small yellow flowers growing in flat-topped clusters at the top of stems which are hollow and often purple at their base. The leaves are compound and are parsley-like.

Although the leaves are edible and can be eaten in salads, one must be careful of exact identification since some of the wild varieties are said to be poisonous.

SALSIFY

Salsify is also called Goat Dandelion or Goatsbeard and is easy to identify because of its unique appearance. It is a pale yellow flower with long outer petals and short inner ones, but is mainly distinguished by the long green bracts which extend a considerable distance beyond the petals. Another unique feature is its seed head which resembles that of the dandelion but is very much larger, up to 4 inches across. The seeds have long white feathery wings and this has led to the name of Goatsbeard.

The flower grows in medium moist soil in open fields, in meadows, and along roadsides. The tap root is edible and is said by some to taste like parsley while others think it tastes like oysters. An extract of the root has been used as a remedy for indigestion.

SNEEZEWEED

Family - Sunflower Family
Botanical name - *Helenium*
Season - July to September

Description -
  The plant grows 2-4 feet in height and has stout stalks. Flowers are 2-3 inches across and have 1 inch raised central disks. The orange petals, which show a decided droop, have 3 teeth at the tip. Leaves are alternate, oval to lance-shaped, and are toothed.

ST. JOHNS WORT

Family - St. Johnswort Family
Botanical name - *Hypericum*
Season - July to September

Description -
  The flowers, which grow at the top of a branched stem, are 3/4 inch across and have 5 bright yellow petals and many long stamens. Leaves are dull green, opposite in pairs, and about 1 inch long. There are many very tiny black dots around the leaf margin.

SNEEZEWEED

Orange Sneezeweed is a common summer meadow flower and is easily recognized by its orange color, its resemblance to a sunflower, and its drooping petals. The plant is large, growing to 4 feet, and produces several stout, leafy stems. At the end of the stems are the flower heads which have raised central disks and yellow-orange petals.

Sneezeweed has a fairly strong odor which causes some people to sneeze, hence the name. It contains a chemical (dugoldin) which can be poisonous to sheep and if the plant is heavily grazed causes an illness that is called "spewing sickness".

Navajos chewed the root as a form of chewing gum and made an extract of the root which was thought to be helpful for stomach ailments. Other American Indians produced a yellow dye from the flowers.

ST. JOHNS WORT

This plant has been made famous by the herbalists who have advertised it as a remedy for a variety of ailments. It is sometimes called Southwestern St. Johnswort or Klamathweed and while not abundant, nevertheless is found throughout the Southwest and is a pretty and distinctive flower. The unusual name derives from the fact that in Europe the flower begins to bloom near the time of the summer solstice (around June 21), close to the date celebrated by early Christians as the feast day of John the Baptist.

It is of medium height, 1-2 feet, and at the top of a branched stem are the dainty yellow, star-like flowers with long stamens. If you look very closely, you will find there are tiny black dots around the margins of the leaves. Holding a leaf up to the light will reveal many translucent dots scattered over the surface.

Settlers made a tea from the fresh flowers and used it for dysentery, worms, depression, and bladder ailments. It also was considered a tonic and the solution was applied to cuts and sores. At the present time it is being studied as a mild anti-depressant and one of its chemicals, hypericin, may have anti-viral activity.

SUNFLOWER

Family - Sunflower Family
Botanical name - *Helianthella*
Season - July to September

Description -
The plants grow to 6 or 7 feet. Stems are stout, hairy, and branched. The flower head may be 3-5 inches across, the rays or petals are bright yellow and the disk is yellowish. Leaves are rough to the touch, 3-10 inches long, and are slightly toothed.

TASSELFLOWER

Family - Sunflower Family
Botanical name - *Brickellia*
Season - August to October

Description -
The plant is 1-3 feet in height. Flower heads are creamy yellow, 1/2 inch across, have no petals, and hang down from the stems. The bracts are straw-colored and striped with green. Leaves are 1-5 inches long, are triangular, and have toothed edges.

SUNFLOWER

Sunflowers seem to grow almost everywhere and are familiar to most people. The mountain varieties, sometimes called Little Sunflower, are very similar to those found in other places but are not as large as the Common Sunflower which is the state flower of Kansas. The large size, hairy stems, large flower head (3-5 inches), and bright yellow petals make identification fairly easy. The wildflower is found growing abundantly in the medium moist soil of open fields and meadows and one variety, Alpine Sunflower, can even be found above timberline. The name comes from the fact that the flower grows best in bright, open sunlight. It has been claimed that the flower heads turn and follow the sun but this appears to be false.

Native American Indians found this to be a valuable plant. The seeds were eaten raw, ground into meal or flower, or crushed to obtain oil. Yellow dye from the flowers and purple dye from the seeds was used in weaving and basketry. An extract of the plant was thought to be useful against snakebite.

Today sunflowers are raised as a valuable crop. The seeds are sold as poultry food or birdseed, and oil from the seeds provides cooking oil and margarine.

TASSELFLOWER

Tasselflower blooms in late summer and is found growing on dry, rocky slopes and hillsides. Although it is a flower and in the Sunflower family, in some ways it resembles a shrub and is sometimes called Bricklebush. The blooms consist of creamy yellow flower heads without petals that hang downward from short branches at the tip of a leafless stem. Each flower head bears a remarkable resemblance to a pale yellow tassel.

WALLFLOWER

Family - Mustard Family
Botanical name - *Erysimum*
Season - June to August

Description -

Plants are 1-3 feet in height and the flowers occur in a rounded cluster near the top of the stem. Flowers are 3/4 inch across and have 4 bright yellow petals in a Maltese cross shape. The leaves are 1-5 inches long, are either linear or lance-like, and are slightly toothed.

YELLOW EVENING PRIMROSE

Family - Evening Primrose Family
Botanical name - *Oenothera*
Season - July to September

Description -

The plant grows 2-3 feet high. The flowers may be 3 inches across and have 4 brightly colored yellow petals. Sepals may be reddish. Leaves are a few inches long, lance-shaped, and become progressively smaller up the stem.

WALLFLOWER

Western Wallflower is a common wildflower that grows in open meadows, fields, and on hillsides. The plant is 2-3 feet high with a loose round cluster of bright yellow flowers and each individual flower has 4 round petals arranged in the shape of a Maltese cross. It appears early in June and lasts through much of the summer.

In Europe the flower was found to grow especially well among rocks and against stone walls and other rocky structures, so it was given the name of Wallflower. During the 19th Century the name was applied to young women who sat on the sidelines (against the wall) at social functions.

Zuni Indians ground the plant, mixed it with water and applied the extract to the skin in hopes of preventing sunburn. Today it is a favorite food for pikas.

YELLOW EVENING PRIMROSE

Although a cousin to the Evening Primrose (see page 67), The Yellow variety, Hooker evening primrose, is very different in appearance and therefore is included here. It stands 2-3 feet high and produces striking, 4-petaled yellow flowers several inches across. The flowers begin to open during the evening hours and are pollinated by night-flying insects. They then often close during the late morning hours.

This plant is called a biennial in that during the first year only a rosette of basal leaves develops. This overwinters and the second year the flower stalk appears and produces the yellow flowers. The rosette is very symmetrical and quite striking.

The wildflower is usually found in meadows, on open slopes, and along roadsides.

American Indians ate the seeds as well as the boiled roots. Tea made from the root was used for colds and coughs as well as for treating obesity and stomach complaints.

YELLOW PAINTBRUSH

Family - Figwort Family
Botanical name - *Castilleja*
Season - June to August

Description -
   Plants are 1-2 feet high and the bracts and flowers are present as a dense spike at the top of the stem. Tiny yellow-green flowers are hidden by the pale yellow bracts. The leaves are 1-3 inches long, lance-like, smooth, gray, and hairy.

YELLOW STONECROP

Family - Sedum Family
Botanical name - *Sedum*
Season - June to August

Description -
   The plant is usually 4-8 inches in height and is fleshy. Flowers grow in dense clusters, are 1/2 inch broad and made up of 5 bright yellow petals which are pointed and in the shape of a star. The leaves are alternate, thick, grayish-green, and waxy.

YELLOW PAINTBRUSH

Indian Paintbrush is described on page 49. It is a familiar flower that appears in a variety of colors: red, orange, pink, lavender, and yellow. The yellow form has a different appearance from the others and many people fail to recognize it, so it is shown here separately.

This wildflower consists of a dense spike at the top of a single stem. The color is found in the bracts which are pale yellow or greenish-yellow. The actual flowers are hidden by the bracts but are tiny and yellow-green.

The general information about Indian Paintbrush found on page 49 also applies to Yellow Paintbrush.

YELLOW STONECROP

Yellow Stonecrop belongs to a group of flowers named Sedum or Orpine that grow in rocky, stony, gravelly soil and therefore are called stonecrop. The fleshy plant, only a few inches high, produces small bright yellow flowers. These appear star-shaped because of the 5 petals which are pointed at the tip.

The flower's leaves are thick, succulent, and waxy, all of which help to prevent water loss and enable the plant to survive in very dry conditions.

REFERENCES

Arnberger, Leslie P., and Jeanne R. Janish. *Flowers of the Southwest Mountains.* Tucson, Ariz.: Southwest Parks and Monuments Assn., 1982.

Bernard, Nelson T. and Dan Godfrey. *Wildflowers Along Forest and Mesa Trails.* Albuquerque: University of New Mexico Press, 1984.

Bowers, Janice. *100 Roadside Wildflowers of Southwest Woodlands.* Tucson, Ariz.: Southwest Parks and Monuments Assn., 1987.

Craighead, John J., Frank C. Craighead, Jr., and Ray J. Davis. *Peterson Field Guide to Rocky Mountain Wildflowers.* Boston: Houghton Mifflin Co., 1963.

Dahms, David. *Rocky Mountain Wildflowers.* Ft. Collins, CO: Paragon Press, 1999.

Dana, Mrs. William Starr. *How to Know Wildflowers.* Boston: Houghton Mifflin Co., 1989.

Dannen, Ken, and Donna Dannen. *Rocky Mountain Wildflowers.* Estes Park, CO: Tundra Publications, 1981.

Dodge, Natt N. *100 Desert Wildflowers.* Globe, Ariz.: Southwest Parks and Monuments Assn., 1963.

Dodge, Natt N. *100 Roadside Wildflowers of the Southwest Uplands.* Globe, Ariz.: Southwest Parks and Monuments Assn., 1967.

Elmore, Francis H., and Jeanne R. Janish. *Shrubs and Trees of the Southwest Uplands.* Tucson, Ariz.: Southwest Parks and Monuments Assn., 1976.

Foster, Steven, and James A. Duke. *Peterson Field Guide to Medicinal Plants.* Norwalk, Conn.: Easton Press, 1990.

Niehaus, Theodore, Charles L. Ripper, and Virginia Savage. *Peterson Field Guide to Southwestern and Texas Wildflowers.* Norwalk, Conn.: Easton Press, 1984.

Pesman, M. Walter. *Meet the Natives.* Denver: Robert Rhinehart Publishers, 1975.

Peterson, Lee Allen. *Peterson Field Guide to Edible Plants.* Boston: Houghton Mifflin Co., 1977.

Spellenberg, Richard. *National Audobon Society Field Guide to North American Flowers.* New York: Chanticleer Press, 1979.

Silverthorne, Elizabeth. *Legends and Lore of Texas Wildflowers.* College Station, TX: Texas A&M University Press, 1996.

Stokes, Donald, and Lillian Stokes. *The Wildflower Book: from the Rockies West.* Boston: Little, Brown and Co., 1993.

Stokes, Donald, and Lillian Stokes. *A Guide to Enjoying Wildflowers.* Boston: Little, Brown and Co., 1984.

Wells, Diana. *100 Flowers and How They Got Their Name.* Chapel Hill, NC: Algonquin Books of Chapel Hill, 1997.

Willard, Bettie E., and Michael T. Smithson. *Alpine Wildflowers of the Rocky Mountains.* Estes Park, CO: Rocky Mountain Nature Assn., ????.

INDEX OF COMMON NAMES -

INDEX OF BOTANICAL NAMES -

NOTES